More Christian Asse

SHARON SWAIN

More Christian Assemblies for Primary Schools

Linking worship to National Curriculum
class activities

First published in Great Britain 1998
Society for Promoting Christian Knowledge
Holy Trinity Church
Marylebone Road
London NW1 4DU

Bible readings are from the *Good News Bible* (*Today's English Version*),
published by Bible Societies/HarperCollins, © American Bible Society,
New York 1966, 1971, 1976, 1989, 1997.

British Library Cataloguing-in-Publication Data

A catalogue record of this book is available from the British Library

ISBN 0–281–05150–X

Typeset by Wilmaset Ltd, Birkenhead, Wirral
Printed in Great Britain by The Cromwell Press, Melksham, Wiltshire

To my colleague and friend, Revd Joy Birkin,
and to the staff and pupils of
St Mary's and St Gabriel's CE Primary School,
Hanley Swan

Contents

Introduction

This, the second book in the series, offers primary school teachers bright, user-friendly ideas to conduct Christian assemblies for the whole school, or for the class, and offers work to follow up the assemblies in a variety of National Curriculum subjects.

Whether your school is a Local Authority, Church Voluntary Controlled, Grant Maintained, Church Voluntary Aided, Private, or Special Agreement school, this book of Christian assemblies is for you!

Christian worship in school

Christian worship in school is a legal requirement of the 1988 Education Reform Act, and all schools, whatever the constituent make-up of their pupils, will want to include Christian worship as part of their assembly time.

More Christian Assemblies for Primary Schools is written in the belief that worship can, and should be, stimulating and great fun, as well as thought-provoking. It offers ideas based on a wide selection of biblical material (not just those stories usually offered to pupils), and embraces different Christian viewpoints.

Many schools have a Christian foundation, and for them it must be an important concern to offer Christian (and in some cases denominational) worship to their pupils. The material in this book is meant to be adapted to suit the circumstances of each school.

This book offers material primarily for Keystage Two pupils. While the 'school assemblies' are aimed at all the school (including teachers and/or parents), some language may need adapting to make it simpler for younger children who are present. Many of the assemblies could also be used with Keystage One pupils alone, providing there is some imaginative adapting of the material.

There are ten themes in the book and each theme is explored through five different acts of collective worship, either for the whole school or for individual classes (or year groups). The themes offered are those that are to be found in the National Curriculum and will be familiar to teachers through their work in a variety of subjects. Some of the themes have already been touched on in the first book in the series, *Christian Assemblies for Primary Schools*, others are new.

More Christian Assemblies for Primary Schools uses the term 'assembly' rather than 'collective worship' (as coined in the Education Reform Act 1988), since most teachers still use the word 'assembly' when referring to school worship. Obviously schools 'assemble' for a number of reasons, worship being only one of these; however, in this book 'assembly' means 'worship'.

Classroom work and worship

For teachers to get the best out of this book, some thought will need to be given to worship and its relation to classroom work.

Christian worship in a school can, and should, be suitable for the age of the pupils. It should also spring from work already being carried out, or initiate new work—across the whole range of the curriculum. It cannot occur in isolation from the rest of the day, despite it being carried out in 'non-contact time'. Neither can worship take the place of Religious Education, though it can initiate or conclude Religious Education.

Each assembly, therefore, has suggestions for follow-up work in the classroom. It is certainly not envisaged that teachers will want to follow up all the suggestions, nor should they replace carefully planned schemes of work. But many teachers may find their imagination sparked so that the theme for the day moves from the assembly into the classroom; they will be able to pick up some of the ideas and weave them into work already planned.

Ofsted inspectors, as well as those conducting Section 13 Denominational Inspections, are looking for evidence that both collective worship and Religious Education nourish the cultural, moral and spiritual development of all pupils. *More Christian Assemblies for Primary Schools* will enhance such growth since the assemblies seek to foster the links between worship and the curriculum.

Worship ethos

Lastly, it must be said that no act of worship will occur if the scene is not set in an appropriate manner. The use of candles, a cross, flowers or suitable music can offer an important focus. Considerable thought is needed as to when notices are given, since this can ruin the feel of any service, particularly if it includes some kind of complaint against pupils. A period of silence after pupils have entered the assembly area can also be very useful, to create a distinct separation between entrance or notices and worship.

The act of collective worship can, and should, be the best part of any school day, whether it is held in the morning, afternoon or last thing in the day. The joys and concerns of the school, and the world, should be allowed to permeate the worship, and this in its turn should infect the whole of school life. An ideal, perhaps, but one worth trying to achieve.

Week 1

BEGINNINGS

As human beings we often have to start things, or to begin again. Beginnings can be exciting, but they can also be very worrying times. This theme looks at what we can learn from other people and helps us to see that beginnings are a normal part of growth and maturity.

A *new opportunity* (school assembly)

New days and new years bring a host of new opportunities. For many children they also bring a host of fears and worries. This assembly looks ahead at the new opportunities that such challenges bring.

Play 'I wish I were . . . !' Ask two or three pupils, and at least one adult, to divulge what person they would like to be, and why. It might be an historical character, or it might be someone doing a particular job (e.g., an astronaut, or a model). Share your own dream with pupils if desired.

Joseph was to have a very bright future. As a young man he was much loved by his father who gave him many presents. Unfortunately, though, he upset his brothers, and had to undergo a very nasty experience, before beginning a new life in Egypt. Genesis 37.2–28:

> Joseph, a young man of seventeen, took care of the sheep and the goats with his brothers . . . He brought bad reports to his father about what his brothers were doing.
>
> Jacob loved Joseph more than all his other sons, because he had been born to him when he was old. He made a long robe with full sleeves for him. When his brothers saw that their father loved Joseph more than he loved them, they hated their brother so much that they would not speak to him in a friendly manner.
>
> One night Joseph had a dream, and when he told his brothers about it, they hated him even more. He said, 'Listen to the dream I had. We were all in the field tying up sheaves of wheat, when my sheaf got up and stood up straight. Yours formed a circle round mine and bowed down to it.'

'Do you think you are going to be a king and rule over us?' his brothers asked. So they hated him even more because of his dreams and because of what he said about them . . .

One day when Joseph's brothers had gone to Shechem to take care of their father's flock, Jacob said to Joseph, 'I want you to go to Shechem, where your brothers are taking care of the flock.'

Joseph answered, 'I am ready.'

His father said, 'Go and see if your brothers are safe and if the flock is all right; then come back and tell me.' . . . So Joseph went after his brothers and found them at Dothan.

They saw him in the distance, and before he reached them, they plotted against him and decided to kill him . . . Reuben heard them and tried to save Joseph. 'Let's not kill him,' he said. 'Just throw him into this well in the wilderness, but don't hurt him.' He said this, planning to save him from them and send him back to his father. When Joseph came up to his brothers, they ripped off his long robe with full sleeves. Then they took him and threw him into the well, which was dry.

While they were eating, they suddenly saw a group of Ishmaelites travelling from Gilead to Egypt. Their camels were loaded with spices and resins. Judah said to his brothers, 'What will we gain by killing our brother and covering up the murder? Let's sell him to these Ishmaelites.' . . . His brothers agreed, and when some Midianite traders came by the brothers pulled Joseph out of the well and sold him for twenty pieces of silver to the Ishmaelites who took him to Egypt.

As we grow older we never know what is going to happen to us. Refer to those who played the game 'I wish I were . . . '. We don't know, but it is quite possible that they *will* become the people they wish.

Joseph was to become a very powerful and famous man. He was eventually to be the King of Egypt's right-hand man—second only to Pharaoh himself. But first he was to be forcibly taken off to a strange country, hundreds of miles away from his family, and treated as a slave. He can't have thought much of this new beginning, even though within a few years he was to welcome all his family to Egypt where they were to live for many years.

New beginnings can be uncomfortable for us as well. Perhaps we don't like starting a new school, or going into a new class, or joining a new club. But if we are to grow and become the people that God wants us to become, then we have to get used to new beginnings, because they might well bring us new and exciting opportunities, as they did to Joseph. We never know what might be around the corner—what a new beginning might bring to us.

 Light a candle as each prayer is said.

Leader: Lord God, we pray for all who have to make a new beginning.
All: Lord, hear us.
Leader: We pray for all who are nervous about going to a new school, and who must make a new beginning.
All: Lord, hear us.
Leader: We pray for all who have to move home to a new place at this time, and who must make a new beginning.
All: Lord, hear us.
Leader: We pray for all who are anxious about meeting new people this week, and who must make a new beginning.
All: Lord, hear us.
Leader: Lastly, we pray for ourselves. Help us to use this week to make a new beginning.
All: Lord, hear us.

 'The journey of life' (*BBC Complete Come and Praise* 45)
'I planted a seed' (*BBC Complete Come and Praise* 134)

RE
Read the rest of the story about Joseph. Create a frieze to tell the complete story of Joseph, and display in the school. Explore other dreams in the Bible (e.g., Magi: Matthew 2.12; Joseph: Matthew 2.13–15; Joseph: Matthew 2.19–23).

Science
Grow plants from pips (e.g. dates or avocado stones). Encourage pupils to suggest how this might be done, and what they might expect to happen. Carry out different trials to test efficiency. Evaluate the different trials after a few weeks and record the test results.

(Note: The best results for the avocado will actually be achieved if the tip of the rounded bottom just sits in water. Push four pins into the stone and rest these on the rim of a glass filled with water. Top up the level of water as needed. After a few weeks a root will appear, and the stone can then be planted into earth, with most of the stone above ground. A week or two later the stone will split and a shoot will grow upwards.)

English
KS2: Give pupils words, or a story-line, to begin some creative writing. For example, 'The removal van pulled up outside the door . . . ', or alternatively words like: 'first day', 'strange', 'funny feeling', 'new' etc. Alternatively, this could be in the form of a letter sent to an old friend. KS1: Give some simple words and encourage pupils to create a story to tell each other.

PE
Learn a new country dance.

Mathematics
Move onto some new work and take time to explore how each pupil feels about approaching new work. Alternatively, 'revisit' work from last term, not to evaluate work, but to encourage pupils to see that they have progressed a long way.

A *new day* (class assembly)

Each day when we wake up, we make a new beginning. We do not know what will happen—what the day will bring. This assembly encourages pupils to see that each day brings fresh opportunities, and not necessarily fresh problems.

Draw copies of the face pictures below. Divide the class into groups of four or five pupils, and give each group the same selection of face pictures. Alternatively, give each pupil a sheet containing all the pictures.
Ask each group to decide what emotions the faces portray. (KS2: Pupils could write the emotions underneath the faces.) Then ask each pupil to decide which face best shows how they feel at different times:

- early in the morning
- on Saturday mornings
- the first day you came to school
- on holiday
- in trouble with Mum or Dad (or guardian)
- when asked to clean your bedroom.

We all feel different emotions at different times. Sometimes we feel happy, sometimes we feel sad or lonely. One emotion we all have occasionally is this one [hold up a large face showing *worry*]—worry!

This feeling is a rather horrid feeling, but it is also an absolutely pointless feeling. Each of us worries about different things. Some of us worry about going to a new school, or meeting a new person. Others worry about going to the dentist, or speaking to someone. We get ourselves all in a state, and begin to panic. But of course it doesn't help at all. All it does is make things more difficult for us.

Our theme this week is beginnings. Each new day is a beginning. Anything could happen during the day. What we need to do is to get *excited*, not *worried*, at what might happen that day, as each new job we do (or person we see), can bring something exciting into our lives. Often our worries are far worse than what actually happens, and we go through all that for no reason!

 Jesus taught his disciples not to worry about what might happen to them. Luke 12.4–7:

'I tell you, my friends, do not be afraid . . . Aren't five sparrows sold for two pennies? Yet not one sparrow is forgotten by God. Even the hairs of your head have all been counted. So do not be afraid; you are worth much more than many sparrows!'

English
KS1: Tell a well-known fairy story (e.g., Snow White and the Seven Dwarves, or the Ugly Duckling) and analyse it for emotions. How does each character feel at each part of the story? Can pupils allocate a face to a character in the story? KS2: Give each pupil a face picture and ask them to use this to initiate some creative work.

RE
Use the face pictures to tell a Bible story to one another, e.g., The boy Jesus in the Temple: Luke 2.41–end, or The death of Lazarus: John 11.

Science
Look at threats (i.e. *worries*) to wildlife in your area, and at positive solutions to help. Threats might be: swans harmed by old fishing tackle; birds harmed by insecticides; animals harmed by broken glass; fish harmed by pollution in steams and rivers.

PE
Look at exercises designed to combat worry and stress.

The first day (class assembly)

Often we look forward to joining a new club, or going to a new school. But the first day can be very different from what we expect. Often on the first day our mind receives a jumble of impressions. We struggle to make sense of a new place and new people, and sometimes these first impressions are not accurate. We constantly need to remember others for whom this is their *first day*.

In the Book of Genesis we find a story ('told by people who lived many years ago to explain . . . ') about the beginning of the world. Adam and Eve have everything they want. Theirs is a wonderful life as we can hear. Genesis 2.8–10, 15 and 18:

> Then the Lord God planted a garden in Eden, in the East, and there he put the man he had formed. He made all kinds of beautiful trees grow there and produce good fruit. In the middle of the garden stood the tree that gives life and the tree that gives knowledge of what is good and what is bad.
>
> A stream flowed in Eden and watered the garden; beyond Eden it divided into four rivers . . . Then the Lord place the man in the Garden of Eden to cultivate it and guard it . . . Then the Lord God said, 'It is not good for man to live alone. I will make a suitable companion to help him.'

Often we have a wonderful picture in our mind of the day we first start school, or the day we first join a new club. But sometimes things are very different, as this game reminds us!

Play Kim's game with the class. Put up to 20 items on a tray and cover the tray with a cloth. Remove the cloth for a moment or two. KS2: Ask the pupils to write down, in silence, the items on the tray that they can remember. Check for accuracy afterwards. KSI: Put up to 30 items on the tray and see if the group can remember the items, together.

The game could be played twice. Have the pupils remembered more of the items?

On the first day at a new school we may meet many teachers and pupils; be taken to a number of rooms or buildings; and be given lots of information about what we should and should not do. The trouble is that our brain gets 'overloaded', and it can become very confusing. ('Look at the trouble we had remembering 20 or 30 items on a tray.') How often have we gone home feeling that our first day didn't match up to our dreams, and wouldn't it have been good if there had been someone there to befriend us?

 Lord God,
Help us to remember what if felt like to be new—
to be starting our first day at school,
or our first day at Brownies or Cubs.
Teach us how to help other adults and children
when they are new,
and never let us forget to befriend others. Amen.

RE
Read what happened to Adam and Eve after their wonderful first day (Genesis 3).

English
Encourage pupils to work in twos and tell each other how they felt when they first came to school: e.g., were they happy, unhappy, excited etc. What was the best thing about the day? What did they do that first day? Pick out key words and use with artwork (see *Art*). Alternatively, start with some 'warm-up' exercises linked to the subject of the *first day*, before continuing with some drama: e.g., a child going to school for the first time (pulling Mum or dragging back). KS2: Improvise some drama on the theme 'The new house'. How might a child feel, and what are the obstacles to be overcome?

Art
In groups, create two large pictures of children, dressed in appropriate school uniform. Place key words (see *English*) around the figures.

IT
Create a banner (preferably on the computer) to display above the artwork, giving your school name.

PE
Explore moods and feelings associated with the theme 'The First Day'. Choose some music, and then create dance or movement to accompany this.

Helping others start (school assembly)

The aim of this assembly is to encourage pupils to be aware of others who may be feeling nervous because they are new.

Role-play two pupils selecting two teams. If desired use teachers to carry out the role-play rather than pupils. Ensure that one 'child' is considered, but not chosen, continually. When all are chosen, grudgingly take the last person into one of the teams.

Encourage the 'child' who is rejected to say what this feels like: e.g., lonely, unwanted, unloved. (The 'child' could be a teacher!)

When we start a new school, or join a new club, we can feel just like ____ (name of pupil who was rejected). It can feel very lonely. Everyone knows everyone else; they know where to go and what to do. For a while we can feel like the odd person out until we make friends and find our way around.

We must always be aware of those who are new and help them to settle in. A new person can bring new ideas and experiences into our school/club.

One man who must have been very worried and nervous about joining a new group was Saul. For the past few months he had been persecuting the Christians, but after a strange experience on the road to Damascus he wished to joined them. Even more nervous was the man who had to go and welcome him. Acts 9.1–13, 15a and 17a:

> In the meantime Saul kept up his violent threats of murder against the followers of the Lord. He went to the High Priest and asked for letters of introduction to the synagogues in Damascus, so that if he should find there any followers of the Way of the Lord, he would be able to arrest them, both men and women, and bring them back to Jerusalem.

As Saul was coming near the city of Damascus, suddenly a light from the sky flashed round him. He fell to the ground and heard a voice saying to him, 'Saul, Saul! Why do you persecute me?'

'Who are you, Lord?' he asked.

'I am Jesus, whom you persecute,' the voice said. 'But get up and go into the city, where you will be told what you must do.'

The men who were travelling with Saul had stopped, not saying a word; they heard the voice but could not see anyone. Saul got up from the ground and opened his eyes, but could not see a thing. So they took him by the hand and led him to Damascus. For three days he was not able to see, and during that time he did not eat or drink anything.

There was a Christian in Damascus named Ananias. He had a vision, in which the Lord said to him, 'Ananias!'

'Here I am, Lord,' he answered.

The Lord said to him, 'Get ready and go to Straight Street, and at the house of Judas ask for a man from Tarsus named Saul. He is praying, and in a vision he has seen a man named Ananias come in and place his hands on him so that he might see again.'

Ananias answered, 'Lord, many people have told me about this man and about all the terrible things he has done to your people in Jerusalem.' . . .

The Lord said to him, 'Go, because I have chosen him to serve me . . .' So Ananias went, entered the house where Saul was, and placed his hands on him.

Lord God,
Help us to remember what it was like when we did not know anyone,
and when we were new at school.
Help us to remember how we felt when we first moved house,
or joined a new club,
and help us to welcome new people. Amen.

'The journey of life' (*BBC Complete Come and Praise* 45)
'My faith it is an oaken staff' (*BBC Complete Come and Praise* 46)

13

➡️ *RE*
Create a list of 'Dos' (and 'Don'ts' if desired) with the whole class about befriending new children who come to school: e.g., 1. Introduce them to my friends. 2. Ask someone to look after them, etc. Put the 'Befriending Charter' up on the wall for all to see. Find out what your school offers to a new child in the way of an introductory pack. Can the class put a welcome card into this?

Art
Make welcome cards to be given to new children entering the school, or class, that include symbols representing the school (e.g., 'River School' might include the picture of a river).

Music
Learn the song 'You are welcome today' (Peter Churchill, *Feeling Good!*), ready to sing it when someone new joins the class.

Science
Investigate the subject of babies. Encourage the pupils to find out what weight and height they were at birth. What colour hair and eyes did they have, and are they still that colour? Invite a mother and baby into class. Discover what babies of different ages can and can't do.

Design Technology/IT
Design proforma to record information gathered from parents as to the abilities of their babies at different ages. Evaluate and correct proforma to reflect the true picture.

A *fresh start* (school or class assembly)

Sometimes we make a mess of what we begin, and we have to start again. It happens to everyone at some time in their life, and it can be a difficult time. This assembly looks at the subject from a positive point of view, to enable pupils to see that there is no shame in starting again.

Play Spillikins (these are sometimes called Jackstraws) by dropping the straws onto a table-top or the floor. Ask two or three pupils out and challenge them to pick up as many of the straws as possible, without moving any of the other straws. Appoint adjudicators if necessary.

Shortly, someone will make a mistake and dislodge a straw. When this happens inform them that the game must start again! ('They must make a *fresh start!*') Replay the game.

Everyone has to learn to start again. There was once a saying that went like this: 'If at once you don't succeed, try, try, try again.' Whenever anyone made a mistake someone would be sure to say 'If at once you don't succeed . . . !' The saying became very irritating, although it was very true—we do all need to try again when we've got something wrong.

We all make mistakes, and do silly things in our lives. We all hope that others will let us start again, without continually reminding us of the mistake we've made. Luckily God understands us and allows us to start again, as we can see from this Bible story.

Naaman, who commanded the Syrian Army, was struck down with a dreadful skin disease and nothing would get rid of the disease. Nevertheless, because of the belief of a little servant girl he was able to start his life again, completely cured of the illness. 2 Kings 5.1–11, 13–15a:

> Naaman, the commander of the Syrian army, was highly respected and esteemed by the king of Syria, because through Naaman the Lord had given victory to the Syrian forces. He was a great soldier, but he suffered from a dreaded skin-disease. In one of their raids against Israel, the Syrians had carried off a little Israelite girl, who became a servant of Naaman's wife. One day she said to her mistress, 'I wish that my master could go to the prophet who lives in Samaria! He would cure him of his disease.' When Naaman heard of this, he went to the king and told him what the girl had said. The king said, 'Go to the king of Israel and take this letter to him.'
>
> So Naaman set out, taking thirty thousand pieces of silver, six thousand pieces of gold, and ten changes of fine clothes. The letter that he took read: 'This letter will introduce my officer Naaman. I want you to cure him of his disease.'
>
> When the king of Israel read the letter, he tore his clothes in dismay and exclaimed, 'How can the king of Syria expect me to cure this man?

15

Does he think that I am God, with the power of life and death? It's plain that he is trying to start a quarrel with me.'

When the prophet Elisha heard what had happened, he sent word to the king: 'Why are you so upset? Send the man to me, and I'll show him that there is a prophet in Israel!'

So Naaman went with his horses and chariot, and stopped at the entrance to Elisha's house. Elisha sent a servant out to tell him to go and wash himself seven times in the River Jordan, and he would be completely cured of his disease. But Naaman left in a rage, saying, 'I thought that he would at least come out to me, pray to the Lord his God, wave his hand over the diseased spot and cure me!' . . .

His servants went up to him and said, 'Sir, if the prophet had told you to do something difficult, you would have done it. Now why can't you just wash yourself, as he said, and be cured?' So Naaman went down to the Jordan, dipped himself in it seven times, as Elisha instructed, and he was completely cured. His flesh became firm and healthy, like that of a child. He returned to Elisha with all his men and said, 'Now I know that there is no god but the God of Israel.'

 Lord God,
Help us to start again when we are wrong.
Teach us how to try once more,
and not be discouraged if we make a mistake,
so that we may move forward once again. Amen.

 'The Peace Prayer' (*BBC Complete Come and Praise* 140)

RE
Read the remainder of the story about Naaman and Elisha's servant (2 Kings 5.15–end). Look up the Jewish Law concerning those who had skin diseases (Leviticus 13.1–46). Although this law did not apply to the Syrians, how might Naaman have felt about his disease? What might Naaman have felt on being cured? Or, go round the class using the words: 'Naaman was . . . ' to explore how Naaman might have felt. Find out about the work of the Leprosy Mission in our world today (see Appendix for address).

English
KS2: Read *The Secret Garden* by Frances Hodgson Burnett. Relate the attitudes of Mary, Colin and Mr Craven to the theme of beginning again.

PE
Carry out some work in the gym that requires groups to move on to another activity every few moments, and to 'start again'. Use the phrase 'Start again' as appropriate.

Science
Investigate life cycles looking at *death to life situations* (e.g., dead-looking seed to established plant, frog-spawn to frogs, or winter to spring). Grow bean seedlings in a variety of circumstances (e.g., in sunlight, out of sunlight, in water, in earth), and take photographs at specific times. Which grow best? Use photographs to create a display (see *Design Technology*).

Design Technology
Design and make a chart to display information gathered about the bean seedlings. Present conclusions (see *Science*).

RE
Look at other incidents in the Bible concerned with starting again: e.g., Saul becoming Paul (Acts 9 and 10); Peter denying Jesus, and Peter and the new church (Mark 14.66–72; Acts 2 and 3).

OURSELVES

In the theme 'Ourselves', the Old and New Testaments of the Bible are explored to look at some of the characteristics that God wants to see in his people (i.e. truthfulness and forgiveness), and some of the characteristics that he would prefer not to see (i.e. laziness and pride).

Truthfulness (school assembly)

Often it is easier to be untruthful. By telling a lie we can get ourselves out of trouble, or appear to be a better person. Unfortunately by telling lies we become someone that others cannot trust. God wants us to be truthful with one another and with him. This assembly looks at what being truthful really means.

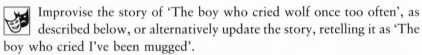 Improvise the story of 'The boy who cried wolf once too often', as described below, or alternatively update the story, retelling it as 'The boy who cried I've been mugged'.

Discuss with pupils beforehand what they think their response would be if someone were to run into the school and say they had seen a live wolf outside.

Then invite a child to become *Peter*, others to become *villagers* (or use the whole school as the villagers), and one or two to act as *wolves*. Inform Peter that he is to run into the room with the news that he has seen a wolf in the forest. Everyone else is to scream and generally appear scared. Peter, finding this very funny, laughs at their panic. The villagers are disgusted.

Allow this to happen twice more. The second time the villagers are only just persuaded by Peter. Again he admits it is a 'joke'.

The third time Peter enters, having seen the real wolf, no one believes him. Behind him come the wolves, howling, as he runs out of the room in terror.

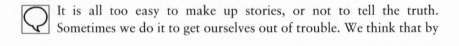 It is all too easy to make up stories, or not to tell the truth. Sometimes we do it to get ourselves out of trouble. We think that by

telling a lie ('It wasn't me that did it, Miss, honestly!'), we will escape the consequences and not get told off. Sometimes this works, so next time we try it again. But eventually we always get found out, and then people begin to stop trusting us because they never know when we are telling the truth or when we are telling a lie.

Sometimes we tell lies because we want to appear big before our friends. If this works we try it the next time. But again in the end people begin to realize, as with the story of Peter, that they cannot trust what we say.

 The reading today is from Psalm 119. In it we see a young man asking God to help him live the kind of life that God wants. Psalm 119.9–12* (or 9–16):

How can a young man keep his life pure?
By obeying your commands.
With all my heart I try to serve you;
keep me from disobeying your commandments.
I keep your law in my heart,
so that I will not sin against you.
I praise you, O Lord;
teach me your ways.*
I will repeat aloud
all the laws you have given.
I delight in following your commands
more than in having great wealth.
I study your instructions;
I examine your teachings.
I take pleasure in your laws;
your commands I will not forget.

 'A still small voice' (*BBC Complete Come and Praise* 96)
'Spirit of God' (*BBC Complete Come and Praise* 63)

Light a different candle for each bidding, and encourage 'eyes-open prayer'.

Leader: God, forgive us for the times we have hurt you by our behaviour. Lord God,
All: forgive us.
Leader: God, forgive us for the times we have let ourselves down through what we have said. Lord God,

19

All: forgive us.

Leader: God, forgive us for the times that we have hurt our friends by not telling the truth. Lord God,

All: forgive us.

Leader: God, forgive us for the times that we have forgotten to be the children you want us to be. Lord God,

All: forgive us.

Leader: God, you have assured us that when we are sorry you will forgive us. So hear now the prayers we have offered.

All: Amen.

➡️ *English*
Read 'The Emperor's new clothes' and explore why the little boy tells the truth, but the adults pretend that the Emperor is wearing beautiful new clothes. KS2: Plan and draught a simple play for radio, based on 'The Emperor's new clothes', bringing the story into the present day (e.g., the Emperor could be a pop star).

RE
Consider if it is ever right to tell 'a white lie'. Try to define 'a white lie'. Look at the way we tell lies to save people from being hurt— about someone's appearance, for instance.

Music
Listen to a psalm sung antiphonally. Read that part of Psalm 119 read in assembly (or another psalm), antiphonally, as a class. Notice the way the lines repeat or re-emphasize each other. Then improvise musical patterns that mimic this style. The music could be used to introduce a psalm at a later assembly.

Art
Create posters based on the word 'Truth' or 'Truthfulness'.

Forgiveness (class assembly)

In our day-to-day life we are often hurt by other people's actions or words. Similarly we ourselves upset others. Often we long to be forgiven, but find it difficult to forgive others. This assembly looks at the way Jesus forgave others, and at what he taught us about forgiving people.

Today the class is looking at 'forgiveness'. Often we do or say something of which we are later ashamed and we wish to be forgiven. Being forgiven is like changing *ourselves* into someone new. We become a new person.

Create simple masks out of card. These could be masks that cover the eyes only, or full-face masks. Encourage everyone to '*change*' into anything they wish (e.g., Batman, a cat or a dog). Templates could be used if desired, to speed things up. (For example, cut out life-size coloured pictures of people from magazines, cut under the eyes and over the bridge of the nose, make holes in the eyes, stick the whole thing onto card, and attach strings. The masks only cover the top part of the head.)

While the masks are being made, encourage pupils to talk about *changing themselves*. What would they wish to *look like* (e.g., taller with brown hair), and what *kind of a person* would they like to be (e.g., friendly). If possible join in the talk about changing yourself—what would you like to be?

21

All of us have to be forgiven at some time in our life, and we all have to learn to forgive others. Listen to what Jesus says about judging and forgiving other people. Luke 6.37–38:

'Do not judge others, and God will not judge you; do not condemn others, and God will not condemn you; forgive others, and God will forgive you. Give to others, and God will give to you. Indeed, you will receive a full measure, a generous helping, poured into your hands—all that you can hold. The measure you use for others is the one that God will use for you.'

 Lord God,
Help us not to judge other people,
and to forgive them when they have hurt us.
Help us to know when we need to be forgiven,
and to ask your forgiveness.
Help us to want to become new people,
changed and forgiven. Amen.

 Science
Link the assembly to growth and change in our lives. Gather photographs or magazine pictures showing different stages of human development. Invite pupils to put these in chronological order from babyhood to old age. Encourage discussion on the signs of ageing (and therefore of changing). What clues are there about age? What control do we have over these changes? Alternatively, look at growth and change in the animal world. KS2 pupils could look at the reproductive system and the main stages of the human life cycle.

Mathematics
Measure the height, handspan and weight of pupils, and relate to the Science work as appropriate. KS2: Produce graphs of the work, and search for patterns in their results (e.g., is age or gender involved?).

Music
Look at different rhythms and their use (e.g., waltz, rap, etc., and improvise simple patterns). KS2: Explore the use of time signatures, or

find out about groups of beats. Look at how a conductor indicates different time signatures (e.g., straight up/down for 2/2 time). Try conducting some music.

History
Investigate changes in lifestyle that have occurred to adults in their own families (e.g., toys, clothes).

RE
Explore the notion of forgiveness. How do we feel when we are forgiven? What do we have to say or do to be forgiven? Do we forgive others? KS2: Look at forgetting and forgiving. Alternatively, read about people who have been forgiven (e.g., Joseph forgives his brothers: Genesis 37–47; the crucifixion of Jesus: Luke 23.32–34a; or the call of Levi and Jesus' work with sinners: Mark 2.13–17).

Pride (school assembly)

Children are often encouraged to have pride in their work, in their appearance and in their school, but there is a difference between this and having too much pride. This assembly looks at what being too proud means.

Look at the following phrases, and discuss their possible meanings. How do pupils think these images might have first occurred (e.g., 'stiff-necked'—someone who is proud and who ignores others might appear to have a stiff neck).

- stiff-necked
- top-lofty
- nose in the air
- stuck-up
- look down your nose
- riding for a fall
- toffee-nosed.

If desired, accompany the phrases with cartoon-style pictures.

Comment that all the phrases describe someone who is proud. Being proud is not always a bad thing. It is good to be proud of our country, of our school, or of some good work that we have done. (Refer to some special work, or activity, as appropriate.)

However, it is not good if we have too much pride—if we think we are better than other people. It can make us unkind to other people, because we are only thinking about ourselves. All the phrases we have looked at describe someone who is too proud.

Jesus told a story about such a person who was too proud, to remind us that we must never become like him: it's the story of the Pharisee and the tax collector. Luke 18.9–14:

Jesus also told this parable to people who were sure of their own goodness and despised everybody else. 'Once there were two men who went up to the Temple to pray: one was a Pharisee, the other a tax collector.

The Pharisee stood apart by himself and prayed, "I thank you, God, that I am not greedy, dishonest, or an adulterer, like everybody else. I thank you that I am not like that tax collector over there. I fast two days a week, and I give you a tenth of all my income."

But the tax collector stood at a distance and would not even raise his face to heaven, but beat on his breast and said, "God, have pity on me, a sinner!" ' 'I tell you,' said Jesus, 'the tax collector, and not the Pharisee, was in the right with God when he went home.'

'You gotta have love in your heart' (*BBC Complete Come and Praise* (alternative words) 87)

Lord God,
You taught us that we should
try to forget ourselves
and to remember other people.
Help us also
not to think of ourselves
as better than other people. Amen.

Art
Gather together a number of different cartoon styles (e.g., from magazines and newspapers, or use clip-art material). Investigate how such artists show characteristics like shyness, anger, laziness, pride, etc. Encourage pupils to respond to this by drawing cartoons of themselves (not of other pupils).

English
KS1: In twos make up a story about a kitten, or other animal, who is proud. Tell this story to others. KS2: Discuss the meaning of 'pride goes before a fall', then read the story of 'Toad of Toad Hall', particularly looking at the actions and attitudes of Toad before and after the car crash.

RE
Read the early part of the story of Joseph (e.g., Genesis 37.3–11). Discuss what it would have been like to live with a brother such as Joseph. How would pupils feel if their brother or sister behaved like Joseph? How much was Jacob to blame? KS1: Alternatively, talk about times when pupils have felt proud of each other (not of themselves): e.g., when someone has won a race, or made something

---

special, or received an award. Pupils may try to talk about the things *they have done themselves*, but gently encourage them to turn the subject back to someone else. KS2: Encourage pupils to tell each other of times when the phrase 'pride goes before a fall' could have been applied to them.

Covetousness (class assembly)

All of us, children and adults, know what it is to want something that others possess, and in moderation (as with the other subjects within this week's theme) it is not a problem. However, when covetousness (as the Bible calls it) takes over our life we lose our sense of perspective.

 Bring a number of magazines and comics into the classroom. Look at adverts for children's toys in these, and talk about the current adverts for children's toys on television. What are their favourite adverts, and what toys would pupils particularly like to own?

It is quite all right to want the things we see advertised on television or in a comic. All of us do that sometimes. But it is not right to want something that someone else owns and to be so jealous of them that all we care about is what they own. We cannot have things that belong to others.

Ask whether pupils have ever watched small children at a play group or toddlers' group—they snatch toys from one another, even when they don't actually want to play with the toys. This is called 'covetousness' in the Bible. In the Old Testament we are told that God gave Moses and the Israelites some rules for living. The last of these commandments mentions this attitude.

The Ten Commandments. Deuteronomy 5.19–22a:

'Do not steal.
Do not accuse anyone falsely.
Do not desire another man's wife; do not desire his house, his land, his slaves, his cattle, his donkeys, or anything else that he owns.'

These are the commandments the Lord gave to all of you when you were gathered at the mountain.

 Use adverts *torn* from magazines to create one or more collages on the theme of covetousness. The activity is to be regarded as prayer, so encourage silence or quiet conversations between pupils about what items might create a feeling of covetousness.

 English
Create catchy adverts that might be used to sell particular toys. KS2: Create adverts that use alliteration, homonyms or puns.

IT
Type up the text of the adverts using different fonts or graphics, and display alongside pictures of the items or by the collage work.

RE
With the group sitting in a circle, pass around an interesting box or pot, allowing each pupil to hold the pot and say the following words: 'I wish for . . . !' The wish must be for someone else. Discuss, or use the material as the basis for prayer, as appropriate. Alternatively, create a wish list for a child in a Third World country.

Music
KS2: Turn the adverts (see *English*) into rap music, and perform for each other.

Honesty (school assembly)

Honesty is about more than not stealing other people's belongings. We need to look at ourselves honestly, and we need to see that honesty does not sit well with a 'finders keepers' attitude.

Prime two or three pupils (or adults) to speak about their lives, where they were born, how many brothers and sisters they have, etc. Included in the information should be something that is incorrect. Then encourage pupils to guess which information is true and which false. If necessary take a vote.

Examples might include:

- 'I was born in ____.' (Mention somewhere exotic, which could be true.)
- 'One day I fell out of a very tall tree and broke my leg.'

Jesus taught us that honesty was important. When he found the sellers in the Temple, cheating the people, he acted immediately. Jesus in the Temple, Mark 11.15–17:

> When they arrived in Jerusalem, Jesus went to the Temple and began to drive out all those who were buying and selling. He overturned the tables of the money-changers and the stools of those who sold pigeons, and he would not let anyone carry anything through the Temple courtyards. He then taught the people: 'It is written in the Scriptures that God said, "My Temple will be called a house of prayer for the people of all nations." But you have turned it into a hideout for thieves!'

In the Temple in Jerusalem there were a number of courts. ('These courts were rather like enclosed play-grounds, but they were for adults.') They were places where different people could meet, and each court was used for something different.

One of the courts was rather like a market place. Here animals and birds who were to be sacrificed were sold. For the Jews believed that it was very important to sacrifice animals. They felt that God would smell the sweet smoke as it ascended into heaven, and that he would listen to their prayers. However, the animals and birds all had to be absolutely perfect. They must have nothing wrong with them at all.

Now although it was quite all right to sell the animals, Jesus knew that the stallholders were stealing from the people. Sometimes the animals weren't perfect, and sometimes the people were charged too much.

Earlier we were having some fun with our game, when we tried to guess who was telling the truth and who was making it up. But in real life we have to be careful that we are not dishonest. We need to be honest about what belongs to us and what belongs to other people: for instance, if we find something, it doesn't belong to us just because we found it. We also need to be honest about what we say: we need to tell the truth; and we need to be very honest about ourselves: what kind of people are we?

There are many times in our lives when we need to be honest, and sometimes it can be hard to be honest, as Jesus found in his life. He was so honest that he was put to death.

 'The Journey of Life' (*BBC Complete Come and Praise* 45)

 Encourage everyone to close their eyes and be still. Say the following words and leave space for everyone to *clothe* the words using their imagination:

Lord Jesus,
You know how hard we find it to be honest:
to tell the truth when we have done something wrong (*pause*)
to look at ourselves honestly when we have been badly behaved (*pause*)
to own up and admit our mistakes (*pause*)
Forgive us when we fail to be honest
and help us to try again. Amen.

RE
KS1: Play a game that involves being honest. For example, prepare 10 to 15 cards beforehand with a variety of questions: 1. What job do you hate doing at home? 2. Name your favourite TV programme. 3. What has made you cross in the last week? Place the cards face down on a table. Invite pupils to pick up a card, and to answer the question as honestly as they can. If they find this impossible, they should 'pass' on to the next person. KS2: Look at the story about Ananias and Sapphira in Acts 5.1–10. What was so terrible about the actions of this couple, and why did they die? Look at the life of the new church in Acts 2.43–47 and compare it with the actions of Ananias and Sapphira.

English
KS2: Write storylines for pupils to complete. The storylines should concern ethical situations. For example: 'Mary and Peter have been

playing. Accidentally a valuable vase has been broken. Peter's mother asks who has broken the vase. What does Peter say? What happens next?' Create the scenarios as drama: draft, revise, proofread and present the plays to one another.

Geography
Carry out fieldwork to investigate the physical features of the school's surroundings. Make maps of the local area using pictures and symbols to represent features. When finished compare them to an Ordnance Survey map and check for accuracy. Talk about accuracy (and *honesty*) in map-making.

History
KS2: Investigate maps and, if desired, map-makers, in one of the Units being studied. (This is particularly appropriate for Life in Tudor times.)

IT
Design a proforma to take some basic information about each pupil (e.g., name, age, hair colour, eye colour). Gather the information needed. Modify the design as appropriate. (See *Art*.)

Art
Create self-portraits (in a variety of media) to accompany the personal proformas (see *IT*), and display. Compare the portraits and information to the pupils they represent, and comment on accuracy.

Week 3

CREATION

Christians believe that God made the world. He may not have made it in quite the way that the Bible describes, but God was there when the world was made, and is still involved in all creation as it exists today. This week's assemblies look at creation in all its aspects, and encourage pupils to see that creation is ongoing.

God's creation (school assembly)

This assembly looks at the world as created by God. It does not explore the issue of how the world was made, but concentrates instead on what the world gives to us.

 Introduce as many items as possible to the assembly that show the variety of the gifts we receive from the natural world. For example:

slate	sheep's wool
a shell	marble
stones	a flower
piece of bark	herbs
root vegetables	sand
egg	coal
fruit	gold
wood	silver
water	

Ask questions that elicit what each item is, where it comes from, and what it can be made into or used for:

wood = paper, charcoal, furniture
bark = penicillin
plants (foxglove) = heart problems
coal = warmth, electricity.

All the items on show are natural products, found in our amazing world. God created this world full of animals and plants for our use. But we are expected to care for the world and not misuse it. It is our job to care for the world's natural resources: to protect the rain forests from being destroyed; to stop acid rain from ruining mountains and moorlands; to protect our seas and rivers from being polluted; and to save animal species like the panda and the tiger from becoming extinct.

Without these natural products our life on earth would be impossible. The earth gives us all we need for a simple life. There is water for drinking and washing. There are plants for eating (tomatoes, apples); plants for medicine (hyssop for a cough syrup); plants to create shelter (rushes to make thatch); and plants for clothing (cotton). Animals give us friendship (cats and dogs); material for warm clothing (wool and leather); and transport (horses, donkeys, huskies). The earth also gives us other essential products. We get oil from the earth which provides us with diesel, petrol, and plastic products; and coal which gives us warmth, light and energy.

As we can see our earth gives us a lot of good things. Today we say thank you to God for all the things he has provided for us.

 The reading today is a psalm of praise to our Creator God, reminding us of all he has made. Psalm 104.1, 5–6, 10–11a, 35b:

Praise the Lord, my soul!
O Lord, my God, how great you are!

You have set the earth firmly on its foundations,
and it will never be moved.
You placed the ocean over it like a robe,
and the water covered the mountains.

You make springs flow in the valleys,
and rivers run between the hills.
They provide water for the wild animals;

From the sky you send rain on the hills,
and the earth is filled with your blessings.
You make grass grow for the cattle
and plants for man to use,
so that he can grow his crops
and produce wine to make him happy,
olive-oil to make him cheerful,
and bread to give him strength.

Praise the Lord, my soul!
Praise the Lord!

 'The earth is yours, O God' (*BBC Complete Come and Praise* 6)
'All things bright and beautiful' (*BBC Complete Come and Praise* 3)

 Ask pupils to come out and hold some of the natural products used in the assembly, encouraging everyone to look at them. Change the words of the prayer as appropriate.

Leader: Lord God,
We thank you for all that you have created.
  All: We thank you, Lord.
Leader: We thank you for slate and stone, for coal and wood.
  All: We thank you, Lord.
Leader: We thank you for flowers and fruit, for trees and vegetables.
  All: We thank you, Lord.
Leader: We thank you for silver and gold, for sand and water.
  All: We thank you, Lord.
Leader: May we never forget all that you have created.
  All: We thank you, Lord.

 Science
KS1: Take the natural products of the earth that were used in the assembly and encourage pupils to use their senses to explore and recognize similarities and differences between materials. Alternatively, sort them into groups according to texture or appearance, and name them.

KS2: Compare the items on the basis of their properties (e.g., hardness, flexibility, strength), and then compare or contrast to 'man-made' materials. Alternatively, describe the items on the basis of such characteristics as appearance, texture and permeability.

Art
Make records of observations on natural products like trees and plants over the period of a week or a month.

Geography
Investigate the physical features of an area surrounding the school. Ask questions like 'What?' and 'Where?' Collect and record rock or

---

plant samples. If desired, create a display about the physical geography of the locality; alternatively, 'revisit' an area already explored.

Music
KS1: Use sounds to create music for the 'Dawning of the Day' (the gradual rising of the sun, bird song, animal noises, wind, etc.), or the 'Beginning of the Day' (bird song, milk bottles, a tap running, a kettle boiling, etc.). KS2: Listen to part of Haydn's *Creation* or learn a new song about the world.

English
Using the items gathered for the assembly, plan and draft haikus on the subject of creation. Present them with the suitable background music, if desired.

RE
Look at creation myths from one or more religions.

Our creation in the world (school or class assembly)

Having looked at the world that God created, this assembly looks at some of the things that humans have created in the world, and gives thanks for our creativity and our involvement in creation.

Ask for some volunteers and create two teams of pupils, with three members in each team. Give each team four small cardboard tubes, a thin piece of card (45 mm × 10 mm), eight books of a similar size, and a small toy car.

Challenge each team to create a bridge out of any of the items given them. The bridge must be capable of holding the car. Inform the teams that you will award the highest points to the team that uses the most ingenuity, and then encourage the two teams to go ahead and see what they can achieve.

Optional: For a school assembly the teams could be allowed to consult different sections of the school as to how they are to carry out the task.

The Old Testament reading tells us about a great act of creation. This is the story of how King Solomon came to build his great Temple in Jerusalem. 1 Kings 5.1–2, 4–6a, 13–16:

King Hiram of Tyre had always been a friend of David's, and when he heard that Solomon had succeeded his father David as king he sent ambassadors to him. Solomon sent back this message to Hiram . . . 'The Lord my God has given me peace on all my borders. I have no enemies, and there is no danger of attack. The Lord promised my father David, "Your son, whom I will make king after you, will build a temple for me." And I have now decided to build that temple for the worship of the Lord my God. So send your men to Lebanon to cut down cedars for me. My men will work with them, and I will pay your men whatever you decide . . . '

King Solomon drafted 30,000 men as forced labour from all over Israel, and put Adoniram in charge of them. He divided them into three groups of 10,000 men, and each group spent one month in Lebanon and two months back home. Solomon also had 80,000 men in the hill-country quarrying stone, with 70,000 men to carry it, and he placed 3,300 foremen in charge of them to supervise their work.

God created our world. He made the sun, the moon and the stars; trees, flowers and vegetables; animals, birds and fish. But he is not the only creator. We can all be creative, as we have seen when our two teams made their bridges.

Ever since we have lived on this planet we have made things. Over many centuries we have learnt how to build bridges to cross rivers and boats to cross the sea; to create windmills and watermills to grind corn; to invent machines like the vacuum cleaner and washing machine to make our work easier.

In our Bible story we heard about someone who was creating a very special building. King Solomon wanted to build a magnificent Temple in which to worship God. His Temple was to be truly amazing. It was to be the largest building that people had ever seen, and Solomon wanted to fill it with beautiful items made from bronze and gold. In the very middle of the Temple was to be a most special place—the Holy of Holies. Here was to be kept the Ark of the Covenant (the box that held the tablets of stone containing the Ten Commandments which God had given to Moses).

As we think about this wonderful Temple that Solomon made, so we thank God for all the amazing things that men and women have made, and are still making, in our world.

 'He made me' (*BBC Complete Come and Praise* 18)

 Lord God,
We thank you for all inventors and creators in our world,
and for all their creations:
for factories, houses, motorways and bridges.
We thank you for those who built cathedrals, town halls and palaces;
We thank you for those who invented computers, cars and spaceships.
Help us not to take for granted all these creations,
and to use them always for good. Amen.

RE
Investigate the building of a local cathedral or abbey church. Look at its shape, its position, as well as outlying buildings. Find out the names of the different parts, and their use (either original or present use).

Mathematics
KS1: Compare objects in the abbey or cathedral, and use standard or non-standard units of length to take measurements. KS2: Investigate the cathedral for specific shapes. Ask questions like, 'Which are the most common?' Look for patterns using certain shapes (e.g., pentagons or rectangles). Record observations made.

Art
Look at old stained-glass windows. Find out how they were made. Look at modern stained glass. How has the style changed? Create your own 'stained-glass' windows using cardboard and tissue paper, to celebrate some local or national event.

History
KS1: Investigate the creation of a building appropriate to a topic studied, or from the immediate locality. Look at the sequence of events from blueprint to finished product. KS2: If appropriate include work on the great builders (e.g., Telford and Brunel when looking at the study unit, Victorian Britain).

English
KS2: Make diaries based on the life of a builder working on the creation of a great building.

Design Technology
Design and build model buildings out of assorted materials (tubes, tins, straws, cardboard, etc.). Allow pupils to choose from a number of options: e.g., a tall and narrow house, a bridge with houses above, a church with a tall spire. Compare different techniques used and evaluate for strengths and weaknesses.

We are part of creation (class assembly)

Human beings are marvellous creations. No two people are the same, even identical twins have their differences. We all have different abilities, different memories and different interests. We are God's ultimate creations!

 Ask pupils to decide which of the following list are the most important to their lives:

- brain
- feet
- hands
- eyes
- ears
- mouth.

Encourage them to share the results with one another. Be sensitive to family situations, and to children who are physically challenged in any way, but do not avoid the subject.

Then look at a variety of situations where different attributes might be needed. Pupils might like to suggest what parts of the body might be of most use. For example:

- an adult falls from a cliff (the voice and eyes may be particularly important to see if they are alive, and the feet to go and get help)
- a child pursued by an animal
- a child gets stuck up a tree
- an adult has a small child who is ill.

We are very complex creatures; *most of us* can use our bodies to carry out many tasks. For instance, we can walk, run and hop, using our feet and legs; we can carry out very complex operations with our fingers (e.g., hold a tiny needle or undo a screw); our ears can hear both loud and soft noises, as well as high or low sounds; and our eyes can distinguish between different colours as well as different sizes of objects. We are truly amazing creatures!

We must never forget that it is God who gives us our different abilities. The writer of this psalm reminds us that we must thank God for all that he has done for us. Psalm 8.1–2a, 3–9:

O Lord, our Lord,
your greatness is seen in all the world!
Your praise reaches up to the heavens;
it is sung by children and babies . . .

When I look at the sky, which you have made,
at the moon and the stars, which you
set in their places—
what is man, that you think of him;
mere man, that you care for him?

Yet you made him inferior only to yourself;
you crowned him with glory and honour.
You appointed him ruler over all creation;
sheep and cattle, and the wild animals too;
the birds and the fish
and the creatures in the seas.

O Lord, our Lord,
your greatness is seen in all the world!

 Encourage the pupils to be silent for a moment and to think about all the different things they are capable of doing. In the silence mention some of these (running, waving, listening, looking, etc.), leaving space for pupils to think about each one. Finish with some simple words of thanks to God for all that he has given us.

→ *PE*
Play a game that involves using different parts of the body, for example, a game of chase that involves running as well as dodging and avoiding others.

Art
Take hand or foot prints using different media, and create pictures or collages.

Mathematics
Investigate differences between pupils (e.g., height, or hand and foot size), using standard or non-standard measurements.

English
Create compound words out of the following body-parts: hand (e.g., handsome), foot (e.g., football), nail (nail-biting), hair (hair-raising), etc. KS1: Give the compound words in picture form.

RE
Look at some of the miracles in the Gospels where Jesus heals the deaf, blind or lame (e.g., Matthew 9.27–31; Matthew 9.32–34; Luke 13.10–13; Luke 17.11–19).

We create (school assembly)

As we have seen this week we are God's ultimate creation. But as well as being amazing creatures, because we can run and talk, and see and listen, we can also take part in God's creation in another way. Like God, we too can be creative. Today's assembly looks at some of the ways in which *we* are creative.

Invite two or three pupils to share with everyone ways in which they are creative (e.g., artwork, dance, music, cookery). Ask pupils of all ages and different abilities. Try to keep the work truly creative as opposed to imitative (e.g., ask someone to play a piece of their own music). You might like to warn pupils so that they can bring items they have made into school.

Alternatively, invite one or more adults to speak about their own creativity. This could be anything (e.g., model-making, patchwork quilts, writing books, painting pictures).

Throughout the Bible we see men and women using their creative powers. Sometimes these are used in the wrong way, for instance, when they make a golden calf and worship that instead of God. In today's story, we see the Israelites making the Covenant Box, that is, the box in which they will keep the tablets of stone upon which are written the Ten Commandments. Exodus 25.10–22:

> The Lord said to Moses . . . 'Make a box out of acacia-wood, 110 centimetres long, 66 centimetres wide, and 66 centimetres high. Cover it

with pure gold inside and out and put a gold border all round it. Make four carrying-rings of gold for it and attach them to its four legs, with two rings on each side. Make carrying-poles of acacia-wood and cover them with gold and put them through the rings on each side of the box. The poles are to be left in the rings and must not be taken out. Then put in the box the two stone tablets that I will give you, on which the commandments are written.

'Make a lid of pure gold, 110 centimetres long and 66 centimetres wide. Make two winged creatures of hammered gold, one for each end of the lid. Make them so that they form one piece with the lid. The winged creatures are to face each other across the lid, and their outspread wings are to cover it. Put the two stone tablets inside the box and put the lid on top of it. I will meet you there, and from above the lid between the two winged creatures I will give you all my laws for the people of Israel.'

God gave us the ability to be creative. Whatever our age we enjoy making things. When we are young we draw pictures, make towers out of bricks, and build sandcastles on the beach. As we get older we create more and more things—perhaps we cook, build gardens, or write computer programs. The ultimate act of creation is, of course, to give birth to a child.

Today we thank God for our creative powers (e.g., the use of our hands—to draw and paint, to model and build; or the use of our brain—to create words and stories, to add up numbers and work out puzzles).

 Create a litany on the lines of the following, adding as many items created by the children (or by teachers) as desired.

Leader: Lord God, we thank you that you make us to be creative people.
All: We thank you, Lord.
Leader: Lord God, we thank you for hands
—that can paint,
—that can write.
All: We thank you, Lord.
Leader: Lord God we thank you for feet
—that can run,
—that can hold us up all day.
All: We thank you, Lord.
Leader: Lord God . . .

'Praise the Lord in everything' (*BBC Complete Come and Praise* 33)

English

Talk about codes. What codes are used in everyday life (e.g., bar codes)? Why do we need codes? When were codes used extensively? In groups of four create simple codes to send secret messages, a rebus to send secret messages (pictures or numbers that stand for words: e.g., 4 = for, 8 = ate, the picture of a cat with the c crossed through = at; numbers to stand for letters: e.g., 1 = A).

Art

Look at pictures that have hidden messages in them (e.g., the Necker cube, the old woman/young woman); or pictures that are full of symbols (e.g., Hogarth). Create artwork in a similar vein.

Mathematics

Create a coded message: e.g., 13 1 11 5 / 21 16 / 25 15 21 18 / 15 23 14 / 3 15 4 5 (make up your own code). Either give pupils a clue (e.g., A = 1), or allow pupils to discover the code for themselves.

RE

Find out about the making of the tower of Babylon (Genesis 11.1–9); the making of the Ark (Genesis 6.14–16); or the rebuilding of the Temple (Ezra 3–6).

Science

KS1: Gather a collection of toys that work by pulling or pushing. Allow pupils to play with them, and ask questions like 'Can this toy be made to move?' and 'Which parts of the toy move?' Sort the toys into groups on the basis of simple properties, and make further investigations as appropriate, like how many ways a toy can be made to move (string, hands, etc.). KS2: Using cardboard lids (e.g., cheese box lids), cover the rims with corrugated cardboard. Make cogs and gears of different sizes by fixing these onto a flat, wooden board. Experiment with size and ask questions like 'Do the cogs move the same way?' and 'Which cogs work the hardest?' Investigate what machines use cogs and gears (e.g., a bicycle).

Music
Listen to the sounds produced by one or more machines. Respond to these musical elements, and make musical effects to copy or mimic the sounds. Use a variety of percussive instruments.

PE
Working together in small groups of four or six pupils, mimic the working parts of a machine. Use mirror imaging and sequencing.

Creation continues (school assembly)

There is a tendency for us to think that creation is complete, that the world has been made, and God's work is finished. But the work of creation is ongoing. We can see signs of this in our own world, and in our own lives as we grow and improve our skills.

Take a *large* piece of paper and fold it into three (across the width of the paper), so that only the top of the paper can be seen. Fix this to an art easel with large clips, and place it so that no one in the assembly can see the paper. Then invite a pupil to come forward and, using a large felt-tip pen, draw the head of any animal they like. When they have finished fold the paper over so that only the middle section of the paper shows. Now invite another pupil out and ask them to draw the body of any animal they wish. Finally, fold the paper so that the last segment, the bottom, is now showing, and invite another pupil out to draw the legs of any animal they wish.

When this is finished, turn the easel round and uncover the three sections of the picture. It will probably be a very odd picture.

Comment that our world continues to change. God didn't stop when he made the world. Indeed the world was made over many millions of years.

Our peculiar drawing was drawn in stages, and the world was made in the same way. Once the earth was filled with volcanoes and boiling lava, then it cooled until there was a time when ice covered most of our known world. The changes haven't stopped there. Each year our coastline changes. In some areas the land is swallowed up by the sea, and in others new land is gained from the sea.

It is the same in our own lives. We continue to grow and change as we get older. Hopefully, with God's help, we grow into better people than our funny drawing. From the moment of our birth we begin to learn, and we need God's help to grow into the kind of people he wants us to be.

 The disciples were unable to perform any miracles when Jesus was alive, even when a man brought a child to them to be healed they were unable to help. Yet with the death of Jesus things changed. Suddenly, with God's help, they gained the courage to stand up to the authorities, and they had the power to heal those who needed help. The reading today is the story of the first miracle that the disciples carried out. Acts 3.1–10:

> One day Peter and John went to the Temple at three o'clock in the afternoon, the hour for prayer. There at the Beautiful Gate, as it was called, was a man who had been lame all his life. Every day he was carried to the gate to beg for money from the people who were going into the Temple. When he saw Peter and John going in, he begged them to give him something. They looked straight at him, and Peter said, 'Look at us!' So he looked at them, expecting to get something from them. But Peter said to him, 'I have no money at all, but I give you what I have: in the name of Jesus Christ of Nazareth I order you to get up and walk!' Then he took him by his right hand and helped him up. At once the man's feet and ankles became strong; he jumped up, stood on his feet, and started walking around. Then he went into the Temple with them, walking and jumping and praising God. The people there saw him walking and praising God, and when they recognized him as the beggar who had sat at the Beautiful Gate, they were all surprised and amazed at what had happened to him.

 Lord God,
Your disciples were unable to perform miracles when you were alive.
Yet, alone, with the help of your Spirit they achieved miracles.
Give us the belief to know that we too can change and grow with you helping us. Amen.

🎵 'O Lord, all the world belongs to you' (*BBC Complete Come and Praise* 39)
'When a knight won his spurs' (*BBC Complete Come and Praise* 50)

Geography
Explore the way that rivers affect their landscape (the erosion, transport and deposit of material; the formation of valleys, oxbow lakes, estuaries, etc.). Or, explore river or sea pollution: create a survey with questions like 'Is there any rubbish around or in the water?', 'What colour is the water?', and 'Is there evidence of bird or animal life?'

English
Look at words connected with rivers and water (KS1: tide, sea, lake, etc. KS2: source, sewage, pollution, conservation, estuary, etc.).

RE
Look at other miracles performed by the disciples after Jesus' death and resurrection (e.g., Acts 5.12–16; Acts 13.4–12; Acts 14.8–11).

Design Technology
Design and make a number of rainwater collectors (e.g., a plastic bowl, a plastic sheet leading to a container). Assess which achieves the best result. Link to Geography project on pollution above. Alternatively design and make a rainwater gauge.

Science
Continue the study of water, by visiting a windmill or a watermill. Make and record observations on the mill. Ask questions about how the wheels turn, and investigate the use of cogs and levers.

AUTHORITY

Children are aware of human authority from a very young age, but this theme aims to help pupils look at God's authority, and the way that his authority is handed on to others.

Giving commands (school or class assembly)

God's word carries authority. This assembly looks at what God's authority means, and how it can change people's lives if they listen to his word.

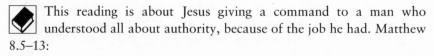 Introduce a game based on commands (e.g., 'Simon says put your arm in the air'. Pupils obey all commands unless the word 'Simon' is missed off the instruction.) Alternatively play a version of 'Follow my leader'. Appoint a leader for a group of pupils. The leader is to start an action (e.g., clapping, arm waving, head-tapping) which is to be followed by everyone else. The leader changes the action every 30 seconds or so.

This reading is about Jesus giving a command to a man who understood all about authority, because of the job he had. Matthew 8.5–13:

> When Jesus entered Capernaum, a Roman officer met him and begged for help. 'Sir, my servant is sick in bed at home, unable to move and suffering terribly.'
>
> 'I will go and make him well,' Jesus said.
>
> 'Oh no, sir,' answered the officer. 'I do not deserve to have you come into my house. Just give the order, and my servant will get well. I, too, am a man under the authority of superior officers, and I have soldiers under me. I order this one, "Go!" and he goes; and I order that one, "Come" and he comes; and I order my slave, "Do this!" and he does it.'
>
> When Jesus heard this, he was surprised and said to the people following him, 'I tell you, I have never found anyone in Israel with

faith like this . . . ' Then Jesus said to the officer, 'Go home, and what you believe will be done for you.'

And the officer's servant was healed that very moment.

This week's theme is authority. The word 'authority' can mean quite a few things. It can mean someone who knows a lot about something—about football (e.g., a famous referee), or about computers (e.g., someone who designs them, like Bill Gates), or about God (e.g., a professor of theology at a university). It can also mean people who are in charge of something (e.g., the Education Authority, or the Health Authority). Lastly, it can mean someone who speaks with authority—so that other people obey them. This is what we mean when we speak of God's authority.

Refer back to the game 'Simon says'/'Follow the leader'. What happened? ('Some of us made mistakes!' 'Some got it right!' 'Some were slow to answer.'). Comment that your 'authority' didn't always work—some pupils didn't follow the commands correctly.

But when God gives a command mistakes like this don't occur. The Centurion in our story understood this. He knew all about authority. As a member of the Roman army he had one hundred men under his command, and when he said 'jump', they jumped! He knew that if Jesus gave a command it would happen. If Jesus said that he had healed his servant then, even though the servant was many miles away, the Centurion knew that his servant would be well again.

God still works in this way today. God has authority to command things to happen, both in the world and in our own lives.

'Praise the Lord, you heavens adore him' (*BBC Complete Come and Praise* 35)

'Somebody greater' (*BBC Complete Come and Praise* 5)

Lord God,
You have the Authority to command the world to spin in space,
the sun to shine, and the wind to blow.
You command us to love one another, and to live in peace.
Help us to obey your commands, and to know as the
Centurion did that you have the authority to change our lives.
Amen.

➡️ *RE*
Look at the creation stories in Genesis. Notice how many times the writer says 'Then God commanded . . . and it was done!' Read the story of the Stilling of the Storm (Luke 8.22–25) and consider Jesus' authority. Compare this story to the ones in Genesis.

History
Find out about King Canute and the popular stories about his 'lack of authority' over the sea.

English
Look at words of command and at their punctuation (e.g., Stop! Stand still! Come here!). KS2: Create drama with the title 'He commanded!'

Art
Create collage work using words of command, with different techniques and textures.

Passing on commands (school assembly)

This assembly looks at how God passes on his authority and power to different people.

🖌️ If space permits, stage a mini relay race, but with only one team. Ensure that there are at least four members of the team and that the 'baton' (or beanbag) is handed on to each runner. The final participant should reach a mythical finishing line. Alternatively, prime a number of pupils and teachers beforehand to receive and pass on a special book. Initiate the procedure yourself, mentioning what a wonderful book it is, and how many interesting and helpful facts there are in it. Then pass the book on to someone else, who looks at it, before passing it on to another pupil or teacher.

 In a relay race the first runner sets off—running (or swimming) as fast as possible—until they get to the second runner where they hand over the baton ('as we have just seen'), and so it continues until the last runner reaches the finishing line.

This is something like the way that God passes on his authority and his power to different people. There are many stories in the Bible that show us how this happens, and today the Church still passes on God's power to people (e.g., in the Church of England and Roman Catholic Churches when men or women are ordained deacon, priest or bishop).

In the Church of England a new deacon is given a copy of the New Testament by the bishop, who says: 'Receive this Book, as a sign of the authority given you this day to speak God's word to his people.'

In the Bible, God's authority is often passed on to others when a man or woman's work is finished. Another person is chosen by God to continue the work. At other times a prophet or king suggests a replacement for themselves.

In this story God tells the prophet Samuel that he wishes to replace King Saul, who has disobeyed him. God gives the prophet his authority to appoint a new king, and he tells him exactly what he is to do. 1 Samuel 16.1–13:

> The Lord said to Samuel, 'How long will you go on grieving over Saul? I have rejected him as king of Israel. But now get some olive-oil and go to Bethlehem, to a man named Jesse, because I have chosen one of his sons to be king.'
>
> 'How can I do that?' Samuel asked. 'If Saul hears about it, he will kill me!'
>
> The Lord answered, 'Take a calf with you and say that you are there to offer a sacrifice to the Lord. Invite Jesse to the sacrifice, and I will tell you what to do. You will anoint as king the man I tell you to.'
>
> Samuel did what the Lord told him to do and went to Bethlehem . . . When they arrived, Samuel saw Jesse's son Eliab and said to himself, 'This man standing here in the Lord's presence is surely the one he has chosen.' But the Lord said to him, 'Pay no attention to how tall and handsome he is. I have rejected him, because I do not judge as man judges. Man looks at the outward appearance, but I look at the heart.'
>
> Then Jesse called his son Abinadab and brought him to Samuel. But Samuel said, 'No, the Lord hasn't chosen him either.' Jesse then brought Shammah. 'No, the Lord hasn't chosen him either,' Samuel said. In this way Jesse brought seven of his sons to Samuel. And

Samuel said to him, 'No, the Lord hasn't chosen any of these.' Then he asked him, 'Have you any more sons?'

Jesse answered, 'There is still the youngest, but he is out taking care of the sheep.'

'Tell him to come here,' Samuel said. 'We won't offer the sacrifice until he comes.' So Jesse sent for him. He was a handsome, healthy young man, and his eyes sparkled. The Lord said to Samuel, 'This is the one—anoint him!' Samuel took the olive-oil and anointed David in front of his brothers. Immediately the spirit of the Lord took control of David and was with him from that day on.

'Spirit of Peace' (*BBC Complete Come and Praise* 85)
'Spirit of God' (*BBC Complete Come and Praise* 63)

Lord God,
You called David to work for you,
and you gave him your authority.
Help us to know what work you have called us to do,
and give us your authority to do it. Amen.

→ *RE*
Follow up the idea of authority as being something passed on. Look at the giving of authority to the disciples (Mark 16.15–18). Explore the meaning of discipleship today—look at baptism or confirmation. Alternatively, invite a visitor to speak about their baptism.

Music
Continuing the line of 'authority that is handed on', investigate the notion of a musical refrain that is repeated (e.g., Fugue from the last part of *The Young Person's Guide to the Orchestra* by Benjamin Britten). Create music with a rhythm or refrain that repeats.

History
As part of the study unit on Romans, Anglo-Saxons and Vikings in Britain, look at the Roman army (e.g., its discipline, standards, laws and the way that authority was conveyed from Rome to the farthest

corners of the earth). Alternatively, look at roads and their importance to the Roman Empire.

PE
Create and play a competitive game with simple rules, where control of the bat or ball must pass from one to another (i.e. authority to play resides with the person who has the bat or ball). Alternatively, play French cricket.

Being called (school assembly)

God calls people to work for him. This assembly explores what that might mean for people who are called.

Invite a guest speaker from a local dog-training centre to come into school with a dog. If possible they should bring a dog with them. Alternatively, ask a local farmer to bring in a sheepdog. Encourage the pupils to be very quiet so that the dog is not upset or confused. Then ask the visitor and their dog to go through some simple obedience routines, including, if possible, response to a dog whistle or voice. The emphasis should be on calling the dog with the voice or whistle, rather than on hand actions.

The pupils could be encouraged to ask the visitor questions about the training of the dog, and how long it took to complete.

The theme today is 'Being called'. Everyone has just seen _____ (name of dog) being called by _____ (name of owner), and asked to do various things.

In the same way we are often called by others. It might be Mum who calls us to come and eat our dinner, or a friend who calls for us on the way to school. Sometimes we are called on the telephone (or the Internet, or the fax!).

Another person who calls us is God. There are many stories in the Bible of people being called by God, just as there are many people living today who have been called by God. (Mention a local minister or vicar as being someone who was called by God to do a special job.)

But whenever God calls it is always up to us whether we decide to answer the call. We can ignore the call, although often the call keeps coming back until we respond.

 Listen to what happens when the young Samuel is called by God. 1 Samuel 3.1–10:

In those days, when the boy Samuel was serving the Lord under the direction of Eli, there were very few messages from the Lord, and visions from him were quite rare. One night, Eli, who was now almost blind, was sleeping in his own room; Samuel was sleeping in the sanctuary, where the sacred Covenant Box was. Before dawn, while the lamp was still burning, the Lord called Samuel. He answered, 'Yes, sir!' and ran to Eli and said, 'You called me, and here I am.'

But Eli answered, 'I didn't call you; go back to bed.' So Samuel went back to bed.

The Lord called Samuel again. The boy did not know that it was the Lord, because the Lord had never spoken to him before. So he got up, went to Eli, and said, 'You called me, and here I am.'

But Eli answered, 'My son, I didn't call you; go back to bed.'

The Lord called Samuel a third time; he got up, went to Eli, and said, 'You called me, and here I am.'

Then Eli realized that it was the Lord who was calling the boy, so he said to him, 'Go back to bed; and if he calls you again, say, "Speak, Lord, your servant is listening."'

The Lord came and stood there, and called as he had before, 'Samuel! Samuel!'

Samuel answered, 'Speak; your servant is listening!'

 'I listen and I listen' (*BBC Complete Come and Praise* 60)

 Lord God,
You called Samuel as a young boy to serve,
and you still call people to your service today.
We pray for those who are called,
that they will listen and answer your call.
For ourselves, we pray that we may learn
to listen for your voice. Amen.

Alternatively, make lists of people (perhaps living locally, or with some connection to the school) who might be said to have been called by God to do a specific job, and pray for them by name.

RE
Look at other incidents where God called people to work for him (e.g., Abram: Genesis 12.1–5; Moses: Exodus 3.1–10). Invite a member of the clergy in to talk about their 'calling'. How did they know that God was calling them to work for him, and how was the call tested?

History
As part of the study unit on Romans, Anglo-Saxons and Vikings in Britain, find out about St Augustine's call to evangelize the people of Britain. What was his response? Alternatively, find out about a local saint and their call to work in your locality. Where did they come from, and where did they train? How did God's call change their lives? Alternatively, as part of the study unit on Britain since 1930, investigate how the Armed Forces called for volunteers before and during the First or Second World War (e.g., Lord Kitchener posters, King's shilling, peer pressure, etc.).

Art
Use the notion of *calling* to produce some artwork. Explore all the means of *calling* (e.g., mouth/ear, megaphone, microphone, phone, semaphore, internet, fax, etc.), and produce posters calling for volunteers to attend a meeting/club/event as appropriate.

Science
Investigate dog whistles. Why are they difficult for humans to hear? Look at the human ear. Experiment with sounds, to see how high or how low humans can hear.

Giving others authority: 1 (school assembly)

Christians are given authority by God to take the gospel to the world. This assembly looks at what 'being given authority' to do any work really means.

Produce a 'last will and testament'. Ideally this should be a real one, but it could be one made up for the occasion as long as it has all the desired language (e.g., 'I ____ (full name) being of sound mind . . . do hereby bequeath . . . '). A will-form can be purchased from a stationers, which would give the correct legal language.

Read out the will to the assembly. Let the pupils see that everything has been thought about: a trustee has been appointed to look after the children; the house is to be left to someone; jewellery and books have been allocated to another; and instructions have even been left as to the funeral and what is to happen to the person's body (e.g., leaving it to Science).

Allow pupils to ask questions, and explore the best place to leave the will for someone to find when it is needed.

Speak about the importance of leaving a will, because it tells the world:

- what items you wish to leave to others
- to whom the items are to go (comment that if you die intestate, your belongings may not go to the people you wish, and it can take years to sort out the legalities)
- who is to look after the children
- what you want done with your body
- what kind of a funeral you want (e.g., a cremation, burial, which church, etc.).

Everyone should make a will (even children, though this might be verbal, and it is not legally binding on parents to obey it) so that the family know what to do if anything should happen. A will tells others (i.e. the people you name as executors) what to do. It gives them authority to act. Without this authority no one can take anything that belongs to you (e.g., money in a bank account, a house, a train set . . .).

Note that a will should always be kept in a safe place, perhaps in a bank, and the last will is the only one that is valid!

 Just before Jesus died he left a will. It wasn't written down, but it did the same thing—it gave authority. Jesus told the disciples exactly what they were to do when he had gone back to heaven. Mark 16.14–20:

> Last of all, Jesus appeared to the eleven disciples as they were eating . . . He said to them, 'Go throughout the whole world and preach the gospel to all mankind. Whoever believes and is baptized will be saved; whoever does not believe will be condemned. Believers will be given the power to perform miracles: they will drive out demons in my name; they will speak in strange tongues . . . they will place their hands on sick people, who will get well.'
>
> After the Lord Jesus had talked with them, he was taken up to heaven and sat at the right side of God. The disciples went and preached everywhere, and the Lord worked with them and proved that their preaching was true by the miracles that were performed.

 'The pollen of peace' (*BBC Complete Come and Praise* 145)

Use a large globe as a focus for 'open-eyed' prayer. Encourage pupils to listen in silence, but to use their imaginations as you read the following words.

Leader: Lord God, help us to imagine how Jesus must have felt knowing that he would not see the disciples again on earth. Was he sad? Or excited because of the work that lay ahead for them? (*Keep silence for a moment to allow pupils to use their imaginations.*)

Lord God, help us to imagine how the disciples must have felt knowing that they would no longer see Jesus. Were they worried? Or nervous? Or sad at being left alone? (*Keep silence for a moment.*)

Lord God, what do we think about Jesus' last words to go out and tell everyone in the world about you? (*Keep silence for a moment.*)

Lord God, we offer you our thoughts as part of our worship today. Amen.

➡️ RE

Look at any of the following as sensitively as possible: at how natural death actually is—all living things are born and all die; at leaving parts of the body for organ transplantation; at the different kinds of funerals that take place. Talk about what pupils themselves might like to give to their friends and family if they die, and make wills. Encourage pupils to give the wills to their parents, and to continue talking about the subject with them. (See *English*.)

English
Read *Badger's Parting Gifts* by Susan Varley, or *Emma Says Goodbye* by Carolyn Nystrom. (See *RE*.)

Science
As part of the work looking at Life Processes and Living Things, explore the life cycles of insects or plants.

History
As part of work on Victorian Britain or Britain since 1930, visit a local churchyard and look at graves dated over the relevant periods. Or visit a church with memorial stones dedicated to those in Tudor times, if Life in Tudor Times is being studied. Investigate ages, occupations, names and attitudes to death. What can be discovered?

Mathematics
Collect and store discreet data on deaths from your locality for a period earlier in this century (ages, numbers per year, etc.). Draw conclusions.

Giving others authority: 2 (class assembly)

This assembly deals with the issue of evangelism, that is, of telling others about God. Christians have been given authority to pass on the good news about Jesus to other people.

 Create a parcel with a gift inside, to play 'pass the parcel'. Make sure the class know that there is actually a present inside. Play the game, accompanied by some quiet music, until the parcel is finally unwrapped. Congratulate the winner.

Ask questions like:

- How did you feel when the parcel came near to you?
- How did you feel when the parcel passed you and the music didn't stop?
- How did you feel when the music stopped while you were holding the parcel?
- How did you feel when you unwrapped the parcel, but you hadn't got to the middle?

Jesus gave his disciples authority to tell others about God, and about all that God had done for them and for the world. One of the most important jobs that Christians do is to tell others about God.

Remind them how it felt to hold the parcel. Would the music stop so that they could take off a layer of paper? Would they be the last one to get the prize? Remember what it felt like when the music didn't stop.

Well, Christians believe that being told the good news about God is like unwrapping the present that lies in the middle of the parcel.

 Here is a story about someone who really wanted to hear about God. Luke 10.38–42:

As Jesus and his disciples went on their way, he came to a village where a woman named Martha welcomed him into her home. She had a sister named Mary, who sat down at the feet of the Lord and listened to his teaching. Martha was upset over all the work she had to do, so she came and said, 'Lord, don't you care that my sister has left me to do all the work by myself? Tell her to come and help me!'

The Lord answered her, 'Martha, Martha! You are worried and troubled over so many things, but just one is needed. Mary has chosen the right thing and it will not be taken away from her.'

Lord God,
We thank you for all that you teach us about yourself.
Help us to listen and learn,
and teach us what to say to other people
when they ask about you. Amen.

English
KS1: In pairs make up a 'good news' message to be taken by a girl or boy to someone else (e.g., a friend in hospital is getting better). Use this for improvised drama, if appropriate. During the day ask pupils to take messages to other teachers—give them authority to deliver the message. KS2: Look at the role of the messenger in ancient mythology.

RE
Find out about missionary organizations (e.g., SPCK, USPG, SAMS, CMS). Look at past and present practices (see Useful Addresses at the end of this book). Investigate material produced by different churches for children. KS2: Investigate which Christian churches have an evangelistic emphasis and find out how this is reflected in their church building (e.g., churches which emphasize preaching and teaching usually see the place of the pulpit as central, whereas those churches that emphasize the sacraments emphasize the position of the altar).

Geography
Use a map or globe to discover where some of the missionary organizations work in the world (see *RE*). Find out about the people and their culture. (See Oxfam or Christian Aid for more information.)

LISTENING

The skill of listening is a skill that everyone needs to learn. Part of the skill is to realize that there are sounds to which we can listen. This week's theme reminds us that we need to listen to our world, to ourselves and others, and to God.

Listening to the world (school assembly)

In a world full of noise we are all losing the skill of listening. We only identify those sounds we want to hear. When our attention is drawn to certain sounds, only then do we become aware that we have not actually heard them until our attention was called to them. This assembly shows us how acute our hearing can be—we can actually define a great number of different sounds with relative ease—and encourages us to try to listen to what our world is really saying.

Gather at least ten items that could make some kind of sound (e.g., a cup and spoon, a musical instrument, two stones, keys, a toy that squeaks). Place these behind a screen and ask two pupils to help create the noises. See how many of the sounds can be identified correctly. Guesses could be marked up on a board and checked afterwards.

If there are any pupils who are hard of hearing add sounds specifically for them, sounds that you know they can hear and distinguish.

Alternatively, invite a piano tuner in to start work tuning a piano. Or ask a child to tune a stringed instrument. How many children can identify the difference in sounds that the ears of those tuning the instrument can hear?

Unless we are stone deaf, we all hear very many noises in our daily lives. From the moment that we open our eyes, we hear sounds (e.g., bird song in the morning, milk bottles being delivered, knives and forks being laid on a table, a radio playing, a kettle boiling), yet many of these sounds we do not notice. It is as though we wipe them out of our brains. We only hear what we want to hear.

Listening requires great skill. It is not something that we can just do, we have to learn how to listen. The man or woman who tunes a piano takes years to learn how to do the job. They have to be able to tell the difference between notes that are almost the same. (Refer to any pupils who are learning stringed instruments and who have to tune them.)

God gave us a wonderful gift—ears to hear—but unfortunately we don't use them as well as we might. We may hear our own names when they are called; we may hear when someone calls us to come in for dinner; and we may hear a siren when it rings. But do we hear all the wonderful things in our world (mention any sounds in your vicinity that often go unnoticed: e.g., the sound of the sea at night, the song of the blackbird in the morning, the rustle of the wind through the trees in spring, the buzz of the bees in summer, or the bursting of the broom pods in high summer) above the sound from the television, computer or cd?

 Hearing is one of the greatest gifts we have. Because we can hear, we can learn to speak. If a person is born deaf it becomes very difficult to learn to speak. Here is a story about Jesus healing someone who is a deaf-mute. Mark 7.31–36a:

> Jesus then left the neighbourhood of Tyre and went on through Sidon to Lake Galilee, going by way of the territory of the Ten Towns. Some people brought him a man who was deaf and could hardly speak, and they begged Jesus to place his hands on him. So Jesus took him off alone, away from the crowd, put his fingers in the man's ears, spat, and touched the man's tongue. Then Jesus looked up to heaven, gave a deep groan, and said to the man, 'Ephphatha,' which means, 'Open up!'
>
> At once the man was able to hear, his speech impediment was removed, and he began to talk without any trouble. Then Jesus ordered the people not to speak of it to anyone.

 Play a piece of contemplative music, and ask pupils to close their eyes and concentrate for a moment on the sounds that they hear each day, while giving thanks, in silence, for their hearing.

'I listen and I listen' (*BBC Complete Come and Praise* 60)

→ *Science*
Experiment by filling glass bottles with water to create musical notes when the bottles are tapped. Predict the amount of water needed to produce high or low notes. KS2: Continue the experiment, until a scale is created (see *Music*). Write up the experiment using a bar chart or graph to present results (see *Mathematics*).

Music
Use the glass bottles to create some music on the theme of 'The morning' (e.g., sounds to represent different birds or animals, the milk man, etc.). Or find out about bells (e.g., handbells or tower bells).

RE
Read the story of Helen Keller by Carolyn Sloan. Discuss what it must be like to be blind and deaf. What things would pupils most miss if they couldn't hear them?

English
Create poetry about sounds that are heard each day.

Mathematics
Create bar charts or graphs to represent the results in *Science*.

Listening to ourselves: 1 (school assembly)

All of us have an inner voice, which we sometimes call our conscience. But learning to listen to ourselves requires more than simply observing our conscience. There are other ways of listening to ourselves.

 Carry out some improvised drama about a cream cake. There could be one actor, with two voices off stage.

Person walking past shop sees a cream cake. Voices are then heard off stage as follows:

- *Voice 1* comments that they want the cream cake.
- *Voice 2* urges them to buy the cake.
- *Voice 1* remembers they are on a diet.
- *Voice 2* doesn't think that one cake will matter.
- *Voice 1* isn't sure, after all they have managed to keep to their diet so far.
- *Voice 2* comments that there is only one cake left, and that will be gone in a moment.
- *Voice 1* wonders if they have enough money on them.
- *Voice 2* says of course they have.

Person finally goes into the shop and buys the cake.

Afterwards hold a discussion about the sketch. Who do pupils think the two voices are? ('The conscience!') Has something similar to this ever happened to them? Which voice usually wins?

 Our conscience often speaks to us in this way. It is rather like having a voice inside our heads. How often do we ignore this voice?

When we are not sure whether we should do something, it is important to listen to our inner voice, for this is one way that God speaks to us. Often our conscience can be giving us more sensible advice than our friends or the rest of the world.

 In the Old Testament there is a story about Jacob, who spends all night arguing with God and with his conscience. The story imagines that he is actually fighting another person. Genesis 32.22–30:

That same night Jacob got up, took his two wives . . . and his eleven children, and crossed the River Jabbok. After he had sent them across, he also sent across all that he owned, but he stayed behind, alone.

Then a man came and wrestled with him until just before daybreak. When the man saw that he was not winning the struggle, he struck Jacob on the hip, and it was thrown out of joint. The man said, 'Let me go; daylight is coming.'

'I won't, unless you bless me,' Jacob answered.

'What is your name?' the man asked.

'Jacob,' he answered.

The man said, 'Your name will no longer be Jacob. You have struggled with God and with men, and you have won; so your name will be Israel.'

Jacob said, 'Now tell me your name.'

But he answered, 'Why do you want to know my name?' Then he blessed Jacob.

So Jacob said, 'I have seen God face to face, and I am still alive,' so he named the place Peniel.

 'You gotta move when the spirit says move' (*BBC Complete Come and Praise* 107)

 The Leader initiates a time of quiet, leaving space to think about the times that our conscience has spoken to us.

Leader:

In the quiet we think about our own inner voice—our conscience.
When did your conscience last speak to you? (*pause*)
Perhaps when you were tempted to tell a lie! (*pause*)
Perhaps when you were tempted to do something wrong! (*pause*)
Perhaps when you were tempted to be unkind! (*pause*)
Perhaps when you were tempted not to help someone! (*pause*)
Lord God, help make our conscience strong,
so that we may live the way you want us to live. Amen.

➡ *RE*
Find out about someone who seems to have no sense of right or wrong (e.g., Hitler). (See *History*.) Talk about our 'inner voices'. Do pupils find it difficult to ignore their consciences? KS2: Investigate words like 'moral' and 'amoral'. Look at the Ten Commandments (Exodus 20.2–17) and create Ten Commandments for the Classroom (these could be positive rather than negative, if desired).

History
KS2: As part of the study unit Britain since 1930 find out about Hitler (see *RE*) and his plan for a master race. Look at the Holocaust. How could this happen in a civilized society?

Science
Investigate whether animals appear to have a conscience. Create a hypothesis and test for accuracy. What results are found? Or investi-

---

gate tinnitus—sounds in the ear. What is it like for a sufferer to live with this illness?

English
Create poetry on the theme of 'The inner voice'.

Listening to ourselves: 2 (class assembly)

Another way of listening to ourselves is to listen to what our bodies are telling us. Often we ignore what our body is telling us, and this can be a great mistake.

Brainstorm ideas on the subject: 'What do our bodies tell us?' (For example: we are tired; have eaten too much; are hungry; walked too far and our feet ache; uncomfortable because we have put on too much weight; yawning because we are tired for lack fresh air.)

The Book of Proverbs in the Bible is full of sensible sayings. Here are two that remind us about listening to ourselves. Proverbs 20:12 and 27.19:

The Lord has given us eyes to see with ears to listen with.

It is your own face that you see reflected in the water and it is your own self that you see in your heart.

Here is a saying about learning from what we hear. Proverbs 19:20:

If you listen to advice and are willing to learn, one day you will be wise.

As we can see, our bodies have a lot to tell us about ourselves if we listen to them. As the first proverb reminds us, we have been given eyes, ears (and brains), and it is up to us to use them to look after ourselves. But sometimes we can be so busy watching everyone else that we don't see ourselves.

As we grow up we need to learn to take care of ourselves—not to put on too much weight, not to get too tired, not to take harmful substances (e.g., smoking, drugs, alcohol), and to take adequate exercise. Our bodies are wonderful things, but, like cars and other machines, they need caring for. If we don't look after ourselves, who will?

 'He made me' (*BBC Complete Come and Praise* 18)

 Conduct a stilling exercise as follows:

> Sit as comfortably as you can, and close your eyes. Let your arms relax by your side (or in your lap). Now breathe in as deeply as you can (N.B. ignore pupils who overdo this, if possible, and continue) . . . feel the breath go down into your lungs . . . and breathe out . . . (Do this once or twice more.) Now think about your toes . . . wiggle them inside your shoes . . . can you feel where they touch your shoes? . . . And now your legs . . . feel where they touch the chair (or floor) . . . (Continue as required, mentioning especially the neck, which may be tense, even with children, and the forehead.)

At the close, thank God for our bodies, and allow a second or two for pupils to 'come round'.

Science
KS1: Find out what humans need to stay alive. Begin to learn about the right kinds of food to eat, to keep the body healthy. Investigate what foods pupils customarily eat, and create charts to display this information (see *IT/Mathematics*). KS2: Plan a Diary for a Healthy Lifestyle (to include nutrition, exercise and sleep) for a child or an adult (see *IT*).

IT
KS1: Store the information gathered on food (see *Science/Mathematics*). KS2: Collate and store the information on a Healthy Lifestyle.

Mathematics
Create bar charts showing the information gathered on food (see *Science/IT*).

English
Discuss healthy lifestyles, looking at nutrition, exercise, fresh air, etc.
Do pupils feel their own lifestyle is healthy?

RE
Look at what Jesus said about our bodies: Matthew 15.10–20.

Listening to others (school assembly)

Our world is a very noisy and busy place and it is tempting to rush around without stopping to look at and listen to other people. Listening to other people is something we should teach ourselves to do, and it is not as easy as we may think.

Offer the assembly a challenge. Do they think they will be able to hear what you are about to say? (Mention you will not be speaking in a very quiet voice.) Take up some of the challengers, and ask them to join you. Then arrange to turn on a tape of very loud music, preferably in front of where you are standing, and some two metres distance from the pupils. Speak to the pupils in a fairly normal voice, without any excessive clarity of pronunciation, as follows: 'Listening to each other is not as easy as we think, is it?'

Listening to other people isn't always very easy. Sometimes it is difficult simply because there is too much noise around us, as when we are at a disco, or because we are a little deaf. At other times we may hear what people say but cannot understand them because they don't speak our language, or else they have a very strong accent.

However, the main reason we don't hear other people is because we don't really listen. We are so busy thinking about our own thoughts—what we're going to have for dinner, or what we're going to do next, or what we're going to say ourselves when the other person stops talking—that we simply don't hear them.

We need to start good habits to listen properly. We need to empty our minds, so that we are only thinking about what the other person is saying, and not thinking about ourselves. When we meet someone else we must learn to think back to the last time we met—what did they say then, what were they interested in (e.g., they weren't very well)—so that we can ask them about the things that interest *them*.

 Here is a story from the Gospels about three people who had obviously not listened to Jesus. He taught his friends that they must love one another, and that they should not think about themselves. Yet this story shows us that they really had not listened to what Jesus was teaching them. Mark 10.35–42a, 43b–44:

> Then James and John, the sons of Zebedee, came to Jesus. 'Teacher,' they said, 'there is something we want you to do for us.'
>
> 'What is it?' Jesus asked them.
>
> They answered, 'When you sit on your throne in your glorious Kingdom, we want you to let us sit with you, one at your right and one at your left.'
>
> Jesus said to them, 'You don't know what you are asking for. Can you drink the cup of suffering that I must drink? Can you be baptized in the way I must be baptized?'
>
> 'We can,' they answered.
>
> Jesus said to them, 'You will indeed drink the cup I must drink and be baptized in the way I must be baptized. But I do not have the right to choose who will sit at my right and my left. It is God who will give these places to those for whom he has prepared them.'
>
> When the other ten disciples heard about it, they became angry with James and John. So Jesus called them all together to him and said . . . 'If one of you wants to be great, he must be the servant of the rest; and if one of you wants to be first, he must be the slave of you all.'

 'From the tiny ant' (*BBC Complete Come and Praise* 79)
'I listen and I listen' (*BBC Complete Come and Praise* 60)

Lord God,
Help us to listen:
to our parents,
to our friends,
to our teachers,
to all whom we shall meet this day. Amen.

Science

Investigate sounds, in the school and/or outside the school. Use a tape recorder to record sounds heard. Which are the loudest and most frequent? Where are the quiet places in school? Find out about vibrations (see *Music*).

Music

Continue exploring vibrations (see *Science*) by looking at instruments like the violin and the drum. Create musical instruments out of a range of items (e.g., tissue paper, comb, plastic containers, paper, rubber bands, blocks of wood, straws, pasta shells) (see *Design Technology*).

Design Technology

Design and build musical instruments (see *Music*). Attempt to predict volume and pitch. Modify the instruments as required, and evaluate the final products.

RE

Talk about people we like listening to. Practise listening to each other (e.g., ask each pupil to speak to another about their cat or dog, or their Granny/Grandad). Allow two or three minutes, and then ask them to swap over, so that they both speak and listen. KS2: After each pair has spoken, move into fours, and ask each child to stand behind their partner and tell the others what their partner has said, using the first person (i.e. instead of saying 'Mary told me about her pet rabbit', the child will say 'I have a pet rabbit'). Talk about how it feels to 'walk in someone else's shoes' in this way. Was it difficult to remember what they had said?

Listening to God (school assembly)

Most of us want to believe that God speaks to us, yet often we are not prepared to listen to him, and when he does speak we are liable to put him to the test, or simply not believe that it is God speaking to us. We need to be reminded that the God we worship is a God who listens and who answers us.

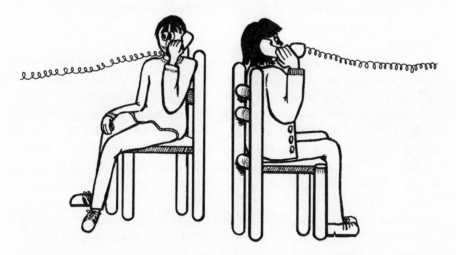

Improvise a sketch with two people (preferably adults), speaking to each other on the telephone. They should be back to back, but at least a metre apart. It would be preferable to use two telephones, rather than mime using them.

A: Picks up phone and dials number.

B: Answers phone.

A: Starts to speak, doesn't say who it is, expects B to know.

B: Doesn't know at first who A is, though the penny gradually drops.

A: Still talking—about anything—though there should be at least two requests, and a lot of irrelevant gossip (e.g., Is B going to pick up her son at school and can she pick up A's daughter; could she possibly let A have a certain recipe; has she heard about ... ; and what about ... ; is B going to ... it looks quite good ... and have you heard what ... said, etc.).

B: Rather desperate to get a word in does try to speak. She asks A if she has heard that ____ (someone in the village) is very ill.

A: Not really listening, simply continues talking. Tells A about her really rotten day—'fell over the cat ... no damage done, though cat a bit quiet ... dropped the shopping ... still husband won't notice that the apples are bruised ... ' etc.

B: Tries again to intervene: 'Has A visited the new family who've just moved in two doors down from her ... ?'

A: Asks 'What new family?', doesn't wait for the answer, but moves on
. . . 'must dash, lovely to talk with you . . . must do this again . . . it's
good to *listen to each other, isn't it?*' Puts phone down.

B: Left holding phone with quizzical expression.

Ask pupils what was wrong with the conversation. Our conversations (or prayers) with God can be a little like this. We do all the
talking, and we don't need God to talk to us. We simply don't leave him
any room to answer—we are not prepared to listen, we simply present him
with a list of what we want. He must be as frustrated as Mrs B!

But God does speak to us. He speaks through other people, through our
conscience, through coincidence (i.e. things that happen most unexpect-
edly), and we need to get used to listening out for him.

One person who wasn't at all sure that God was speaking to her was
Sarah, Abraham's wife. If it was God that was speaking then he had
surely made a huge mistake, thought Sarah. Genesis 18.1–15:

> The Lord appeared to Abraham at the sacred trees of Mamre. As
> Abraham was sitting at the entrance of his tent during the hottest part of
> the day, he looked up and saw three men standing there. As soon as he
> saw them, he ran out to meet them. Bowing down with his face touching
> the ground, he said, 'Sirs, please do not pass by my home without
> stopping; I am here to serve you. Let me bring some water for you to
> wash your feet; you can rest here beneath this tree. I will also bring a bit
> of food; it will give you strength to continue your journey. You have
> honoured me by coming to my home, so let me serve you.'
>
> They replied, 'Thank you; we accept.'
>
> Abraham hurried into the tent and said to Sarah, 'Quick, take a sack
> of your best flour, and bake some bread.' Then he ran to the herd and
> picked out a calf that was tender and fat, and gave it to a servant, who
> hurried to get it ready. He took some cream, some milk, and the meat,
> and set the food before the men. There under the tree he served them
> himself, and they ate.
>
> Then they asked him, 'Where is your wife Sarah?'
>
> 'She is there in the tent,' he answered.
>
> One of them said, 'Nine months from now I will come back, and your
> wife Sarah will have a son.'
>
> Sarah was behind him, at the door of the tent, listening. Abraham and
> Sarah were very old . . . so Sarah laughed to herself and said, 'Now that

I am old and worn out, can I still enjoy sex? And besides my husband is old too.'

Then the Lord asked Abraham, 'Why did Sarah laugh and say, "Can I really have a child when I am so old?" Is anything too hard for the Lord? As I said, nine months from now I will return, and Sarah will have a son.'

Because Sarah was afraid, she denied it. 'I didn't laugh,' she said. 'Yes, you did,' he replied. 'You laughed.'

 'A still small voice' (BBC *Complete Come and Praise* 96)

RE
Look at other stories where God speaks to men and women, either directly, or through an angel (e.g., Elijah in the cave: 1 Kings 19.8–16; and Zechariah: Luke 1.5–25). Explore how God speaks to people today. Find out about prayers in different Christian denominations. How much listening occurs, and how much is about talking to God? Create prayers for use in assembly that leave space for listening. Put these into folders and use them. (See *Design Technology/IT*.)

Design Technology/IT
Create prayer folders for use in assembly (see *RE*).

English
Tell a well-known story (e.g., KS1: Cinderella; KS2: the Good Samaritan), then divide the class into groups. Each group is to take one character (e.g., KS1: an ugly sister or Buttons), and come back to tell the story from their point of view. How different will the story be? Pursue the idea that what people say can sometimes be slanted from their own point of view!

Week 6

LOVE

Christianity is all about love: God's love for his people. This theme looks at what this message actually means in a world that believes it understands all about love.

What is love? (school assembly)

The title of this assembly sounds rather like the title for a song about love—a subject we all, including children, feel we know something about. However, we need to look again at the word *love*, and at what it means to us, to see if we are as knowledgeable as we think.

Do not announce the theme of this week's assemblies, but start by offering a number of riddles for pupils to solve. For example, 'The theme of this week's assemblies is the thing you have when you give it away', or, 'It's not an object and it can't be touched, but we can see it in action.'

Finally, suggest that more people talk about this subject than anything else in the world, there are more films about it, more television programmes mention it, millions of songs are sung about it, and it affects every single human being in the world in some way or other.

If they are still stuck, put up an anagram of LOVE, and when they have worked it out write LOVE IS. Ask for definitions of love. What does love mean to the pupils and teachers present? Encourage any comments (e.g., 'being cuddled' or 'having my muddy boots taken off', as well as 'sex'). Be prepared for those who will want to shock!

Finally, comment that love is all of these things and more.

This is the story of someone who was desperate to have a son. For a Jewish woman, not to have a child was the most terrible disgrace imaginable, and a husband could divorce his wife if she had no children. Hannah wanted a son for her husband so badly that she was willing to offer the child to God. Listen to what happened in her amazing story. 1 Samuel 1.1a, 2–6, 9–19a, 20–22:

There was a man named Elkanah . . . Elkanah had two wives, Hannah and Peninnah. Peninnah had children, but Hannah had none. Every year Elkanah went from Ramah to worship and offer sacrifices to the Lord Almighty at Shiloh, where Hophni and Phinehas, the two sons of Eli, were priests of the Lord. Each time Elkanah offered his sacrifice, he would give one share of the meat to Peninnah and one share to each of her children. And even though he loved Hannah very much he would give her only one share, because the Lord had kept her from having children. Peninnah, her rival, would torment and humiliate her, because the Lord had kept her childless . . .

One day, after they had finished their meal in the house of the Lord at Shiloh, Hannah got up. She was deeply distressed, and she cried bitterly as she prayed to the Lord. Meanwhile, Eli the priest was sitting in his place by the door. Hannah made a solemn promise: 'Lord Almighty, look at me, your servant! See my trouble and remember me! Don't forget me! If you give me a son, I promise that I will dedicate him to you for his whole life and that he will never have his hair cut.'

Hannah continued to pray to the Lord for a long time, and Eli watched her lips. She was praying silently; her lips were moving, but she made no sound. So Eli thought that she was drunk, and he said to her, 'Stop making a drunken show of yourself! Stop your drinking and sober up!'

'No, I'm not drunk, sir,' she answered. 'I haven't been drinking! I am desperate, and I have been praying, pouring out my troubles to the Lord. Don't think I am a worthless woman. I have been praying like this because I'm so miserable.'

'Go in peace,' Eli said, 'and may the God of Israel give you what you have asked him for.' . . .

The next morning Elkanah and his family got up early, and after worshipping the Lord, they went back home to Ramah . . . and the Lord answered [Hannah's] prayer. So it was that she became pregnant and gave birth to a son. She named him Samuel, and explained, 'I asked the Lord for him.'

The time came again for Elkanah and his family to go to Shiloh and offer to the Lord the yearly sacrifice and the special sacrifice he had promised. But this time Hannah did not go. She told her husband, 'As soon as the child is weaned, I will take him to the house of the Lord, where he will stay all his life.'

For Hannah, love was giving away the most precious thing in her life—her son Samuel—to serve God. Samuel was to become one of the greatest prophets of all. Because of his mother's action he was to serve God all his life.

As we said at the beginning of the assembly, real love is something we give away. When we really love someone we do not think about ourselves, we only care about the other person. Hannah cared more about God than about herself, and having been granted her wish to have a son she was willing to give him back to serve God for the rest of his life.

Refer to the 'Love is . . . ' statements, and particularly those that *give* rather than *take*.

 'Love will never come to an end' (*BBC Complete Come and Praise* 99)

 Light a large candle which has been placed in a bowl of sand. Have a few small candles ready to be lit, and ask pupils to think of 'Love to be thankful for' (e.g., parent's love, love for an animal, love for a baby, God's love). Then invite pupils to share their thoughts with the rest of the assembly, before coming out to light a candle. Finally, keep silence for a moment to allow everyone to think of the different aspects of love for which they are thankful.

RE
Talk about the most precious belongings that pupils own. What things are important to them and why (e.g., a shell picked up on the beach when walking with Grandad who is now dead; a teddy they have had since babyhood). Encourage each child to appreciate how special these items are to the person concerned. Try to imagine how hard it would be to give away such a treasure, and how hard it must have been for Hannah to give her baby to God. Create a 'Love is . . . ' list for each pupil (see *Art*).

Art
Imagine what colour 'love' would be and create a picture in that colour to accompany the 'Love is . . . ' lists (see *RE*).

English
Create haikus on the feelings aroused by the 'Love is . . . ' lists.

History
Look at an historical character within the current study unit who showed some special aspect of love in their life.

Loving our neighbour (school or class assembly)

How can we be said to *love* our neighbour, and who is our neighbour? We all have problems with these questions at some time or other. This assembly looks at the reality of loving one's neighbour.

 Give six pupils who are able to read cards with the following words on them. You might also choose to give them large name badges.

1. (*a girl*) I am Miss Williams. I am 74 years old, and I hate children, particularly those who kick balls into my garden, and teenagers who come home late and stand shouting in the street half the night.

2. (*a boy*) I am Martin. I'm 7 years old, and I live next door to an old woman who's always yelling at me and my friends.

3. (*a girl*) I'm Mrs Brown. I'm 30 years old, and I'm out at work all day and want to sleep in on Saturday morning, but those ghastly kids next door always wake me up.

4. (*a boy*) I'm James. I'm 10 years old, and I like football, especially on Saturday morning when we don't have to go to school and I can play outside in the street with my friends, except when one of them next door stops us.

5. (*a girl*) I'm Jane. I'm 18 years old, and I like to go to discos on Saturday night, come in very late, and sleep all day Sunday—some hope in this place!

6. (*a boy*) I'm David. I'm 40 years old, and I do shift-work, and the sooner I can move out of this estate the better; no one does anything but moan.

Ask the pupils to come out to the front and read the words on the cards to the assembly.

Keep the pupils at the front and refer to their *characters* as necessary. These six people all live in the same street, and as can be seen they positively hate one another. Each one annoys the other in some way.

It is the same, however, on a global scale. One country can annoy another, or one faith-group (or 'religious group') upset another. Our neighbour is not just the person next door, it is also the country next door, and the country half-way across the world.

All these people (next door and overseas) are the people that Jesus said we had to love. He taught us to love everyone in the same way that we love ourselves. We need to think about them and care for them, in the same way that we think and care about ourselves. This applies especially when we find them hard to get on with.

As well as this, Jesus also encouraged us to love those who actually hate us. Anyone can love a person who loves them, but it is much harder to love those who hate us.

Listen to what Jesus said about loving our neighbour: Matthew 5.43–48. Alternatively, read the parable of The Good Samaritan (Luke 10.30–37), but explain that all Jews hated Samaritans because they had set up a rival temple in Samaria.

'You have heard that it was said, "Love your friends, hate your enemies." But now I tell you: love your enemies and pray for those who persecute you, so that you may become the sons of your Father in heaven. For he makes his sun to shine on bad and good people alike, and gives rain to those who do good and to those who do evil. Why should God reward you if you love only the people who love you? Even the tax collectors do that! And if you speak only to your friends, have you done anything out of the ordinary? Even the pagans do that! You must be perfect—just as your Father in heaven is perfect!'

 'I was lying in the roadway' (*BBC Complete Come and Praise* 88)

 Lord God,
Help us to love one another,

especially those whom we find most difficult.
Help us to love one another,
even when we feel cross and awkward.
Help us to love one another,
even when we'd rather not. Amen.

RE
KS1: Talk about how difficult it is to like people that do not like us. Does our behaviour change because we know they don't like us? Would our relationship change if we were nicer to them, or if we thought about how they might feel? ('Miss Williams is probably very lonely, and may not have any friends or family. Instead of kicking a ball into her garden perhaps Martin could get to know her better.')

KS2: Play Consequences. Working in small groups, give each group a sentence to do with one of the characters in the assembly. The groups may need to be reminded of the characters. For example, the first person in the group might start with: 'I am Miss Williams, and I feel particularly cross today . . . '. The second person in the group must then add a 'consequence': e.g., 'so when there was a knock on my door . . . ' etc. When all the members of the group have spoken, come to a halt and look at the consequence of Miss Williams getting up late. If the end result was bad, try it again and see if you can change the end result to something more positive.

English
Create 'freeze-frame' drama (pupils create static 'pictures' for each segment of the story) based on the story of The Good Samaritan. If desired, divide the class into small groups. Each group could produce one part of the story (e.g., the man travelling to Jericho; the man attacked by thieves). Put these together with the story, and use in another assembly.

Geography
Create maps showing where each pupil lives, and mark on the maps the houses of their immediate neighbours. Mark in the houses of friends who live nearby. KS2: Widen the maps to look at the

surrounding area. Which villages and towns do they naturally look towards? As a class, transfer the information to a single map, creating symbols as necessary. Do all pupils look to the same villages or towns?

History
KS2: As part of the study unit Britain since 1930 look at helping one's neighbour during the war.

Loving God (school assembly)

What does it mean to 'love God', and how can we show our love for God in a world that all too often only cares for itself?

Ask pupils how we behave when we love someone (e.g., parent, baby brother or sister). Write up ideas on a board under the heading 'Love', but only write on the left-hand side of the board. Ideas similar to the following will probably come up:

• we want to be with them
• we want to help them
• we want to do what they want
• we want to praise them
• we want to care for them.

Then create a list on the right-hand side of the board to show how we should behave if we say we love God. Tease out what they mean if the comments are similar to the first ones. Ideas similar to the following may come up:

• we want to be with him (i.e. go to church/pray)
• we want to help him do his work (how?)
• we want to praise him (how?)
• we want to follow his commands (what commands?).

One man who knew all about loving God was Daniel. Although he lived many hundreds of years ago, his life wasn't so very different from ours. It was still difficult to be one of God's people. Daniel 6.1–8a, 10–12a and 16a:

Darius decided to appoint a hundred and twenty governors to hold office throughout his empire. In addition, he chose Daniel and two others to supervise the governors and to look after the king's interest. Daniel soon showed that he could do better work than the other supervisors or the governors. Because he was so outstanding, the king considered putting him in charge of the whole empire. Then the other supervisors and the governors tried to find something wrong with the way Daniel administered the empire, but they couldn't, because Daniel was reliable and did not do anything wrong or dishonest. They said to one another, 'We are not going to find anything of which to accuse Daniel unless it is something in connection with his religion.'

So they went to see the king and said, 'King Darius, may Your

Majesty live for ever! All of us who administer your empire—the supervisors, the governors, the lieutenant-governors, and the other officials—have agreed that Your Majesty should issue an order and enforce it strictly. Give orders that for thirty days no one can be permitted to request anything from any god or from any man except from Your Majesty. Anyone who violates this order is to be thrown into a pit filled with lions. So let Your Majesty issue this order and sign it, and it will be in force' . . .

When Daniel learnt that the order had been signed, he went home. In an upstairs room of his house there were windows that faced towards Jerusalem. There just as he had always done, he knelt down at the open windows and prayed to God three times a day.

When Daniel's enemies observed him praying to God, all of them went together to the king to accuse Daniel . . . the king gave orders for Daniel to be arrested.

One of the reasons that we love God is that he first loved us. Daniel knew that kings were not reliable—it was much safer for him to stick with God. He knew that God would stand by him, even when all his enemies were against him.

God cares for us in the same way that a good parent cares for and loves a child ('or in the same way that you love your dog or cat'). He sees that we have enough food to eat, he protects us and keeps us safe, and he is always with us.

We show our love for God when we obey his commands, when we want to share what we have with other people, and when we try to care for them as he cares for us.

Note: Don't get involved in the fact that sometimes we are not safe. This can be looked at in the classroom. It is sufficient that God loves us. Ultimately he takes us back to himself at our death, and that too is love!

 'Come and praise the Lord our King' (*BBC Complete Come and Praise* 21)

'Now thank we all our God' (*BBC Complete Come and Praise* 38)

 Leader: When we think of Jesus Christ,
      All: we are loving you, Lord God.
Leader: When we remember others across the world who need our help,

All: we are loving you, Lord God.
Leader: When we are kind to our neighbour or friend,
All: we are loving you, Lord God.
Leader: When we obey your commands,
All: we are loving you, Lord God. Amen.

▶ *RE*
Read the remainder of Daniel's story, of how he survives being put into the lions' den, and of what happens to the king (Daniel 6.16–28). Alternatively, read the story of The Lost Son (Luke 15.11–32) and talk about God's love for his people. Find out about people who have shown their love for God in the way they help others (e.g., Gladys Aylward, Dr Barnardo, Robert Raikes, Mother Teresa, or someone living locally).

Geography
Find out about Traidcraft and Fairtrade (see Useful Addresses). Investigate lifestyles in India or South America, and the obstacles to Fair Trade. Find out where some of our staple foods come from (e.g., coffee, tea, beans). Collect a normal week's selection of food and mark countries of origin on a map.

Mathematics
Compare incomes and a normal week's shopping costs in a developing country to that in this country. What are the differences?

English
KS2: How would Daniel have felt when the king decided that no one should worship anyone but him? Would Daniel have contemplated agreeing to the law? Write a letter from Daniel to some friends still in Jerusalem, telling them of his dilemma.

Loving ourselves (class assembly)

Many people do not *like* themselves, yet we need to *love* ourselves if we are to love other people. Somehow we need to strike a balance between being too fond of ourselves and feeling we are not worth anything. In our world today many people have swung from one extreme to the other, and we need to help pupils see that the extremes are not desirable.

 Ask a girl to read the 'I hate myself' rap to suitable percussion music. Alternatively, read the rap yourself.

\It was morning \in the playground \when the new boy \came by,
\He was cool, \he was hip, and I \felt that I would \die.
\Would he notice, \would he see me?— \I really couldn't \tell—
for he \rushed right \past me as the \teacher rang the \bell.

\'Welcome to St \Joseph's!' I \stammered, with a \smile—
as he coll\ided with the \doorpost, and \landed in a \pile.
\'Nice one!' he muttered \darkly, his \face filled with \hate—
'There's \always one! Stay \there! Don't \ask to be my \date.'

'As If I \would, the cheek of \it, who \did he think he \was—
Arnie \Swartz, Michael \Jackson, or a \member of the \Broz?
I \sniffed, and turned my \head. He could \certainly get \lost!
I'd \better things to \do, and \sure would not be \bossed!

At \break-time it was \wet, and we \hung out near the \door.
What \was his name? Where \did he live? It \really was a \bore—
I \could not see him \anywhere. He \must have gone, I \feared.
He was \nowhere to be \seen—he'd com\pletely disa\ppeared.

Then a \voice said \'Hi there! Have we \met be\fore?—
Is it \you? Oh! \No! The one who \threw me on the \floor.
No o\ffence, but \'*Move!*' 'A\llow me to \pass!'
And he \pushed right \by me as \bold as \brass.

'A\llow me to \help you!' I \gave an evil \grin—
He \tripped on my \bag, and was \kicked in the \shin.
He \backed away in \horror, 'What \have we got \here—
Are you \Frankenstein, or \Dracula?' he \asked in great \fear.

It was \late when I got \home, and the \house was very \still.
I \crashed out on the \bed, feeling \very, very \ill.

'I \hate myself! I \hate myself!' was \my continual \cry
\Buried under \blankets I \wished that I could \die.

(*pause*)

To\morrow in the \playground when the \new boy comes \by,
I'll be \cool, I'll be \hip, and I \know that he will \cry:
\'Come and watch the \football? I'll \walk you \back'—
And I \just might \answer, 'I'll \wait near the \track.'

After listening to the rap, organize the class into twos, and ask them to tell each other, in turn, what they like about each other (e.g., colour of hair, smiling eyes, kindness, good at football).

 Psalm 8 reminds us that God made us *second to himself*. So how dare we put ourselves down, if God thinks so much of us? Psalm 8.1a, 4–5:

O Lord, our Lord,
your greatness is seen in all the world! . . .
what is man, that you think of him;
mere man, that you care for him?

Yet you made him inferior only to yourself;
you crowned him with glory and honour.

We cannot expect to love other people if we don't love ourselves. We need to believe in ourselves, tell ourselves we can do something, and learn to feel good about our minds and our bodies. The girl in the rap had a real problem. Perhaps she should have got up each morning, looked in the mirror and said, 'God loves you, so love yourself!' Then she wouldn't have hated herself, even after such a bad day.

Also, God thinks a lot of us. He made us, and he loves us. We are, after all, his creations. So if God cares for us, we should care for ourselves.

 Lord God,
We thank you for our hair (*pause*)
our eyes (*pause*)
our faces (*pause*)
our bodies (*pause*)
our personalities (*pause*)
May we appreciate ourselves, as we are. Amen.

➡️ *Art*
Draw portraits, picking out the best features of each person.

English
Create word lists of positive words to say about each other.

RE
Play 'If I were a ____ I would be a ____ ' in pairs (e.g., a colour, a flower, a car), and in a larger group gently tease out meanings. Encourage pupils to be honest rather than boastful.

Loving God's creatures (school or class assembly)

One of our responsibilities is to love and care for other species in our world. We live in the world as stewards, that is, people responsible for the whole world—for all its animals, plants and fish, as well as all its people.

◆ Invite one or two parents or pupils to bring a pet animal into school. This could be a small animal like a hamster, a gerbil or a goldfish, or a larger one like a cat or dog. (If this is a classroom assembly use a small animal.)

Lay down some simple rules about caring for the animals while they are in the classroom or hall, to ensure that the animals are not nervous (e.g., keep quiet, only one pupil—or the owner—to handle the animal).

Then ask the owner questions about caring for the animal (e.g., what food does it eat, how much exercise does it need, how much does it drink, what are the difficulties of looking after the animal). Encourage pupils in the assembly to ask their own questions.

◆ Read the story of the lost sheep. This parable is actually about God searching out one sinner that is lost, but it is also a good example of how shepherds in Palestine cared for their sheep, for they were very valuable to them. Luke 15.4–6:

'Suppose one of you has a hundred sheep and loses one of them—what does he do? He leaves the other ninety-nine sheep in the pasture and goes looking for the one that got lost until he finds it. When he finds it, he is so happy that he puts it on his shoulders and carries it back home. Then he calls his friends and neighbours together and says to them "I am so happy I found my lost sheep, Let us celebrate!"'

We are called by God to care for all his creatures—indeed, for his whole world. We live in the world merely as 'caretakers', ready to hand on our responsibilities to the next generation. The whole earth belongs not to us, but to God (see Psalm 24.1), and we look after it for him (see Psalm 8.6–8). So it is up to each one of us to look after all the animals, birds, fish and plants on our earth, and make sure that we have a healthy world to hand on to those who come after us.

This means that it is very important that we make sure that we do not pollute the world; that we save species that are threatened with extinction; that we care for all God's creatures, no matter how big or small they are. God asks us to love and care for all his creatures.

 Read Psalm 24.1:

The world and all that is in it
belong to the Lord;
the earth and all who live on it are his.

Then pray:

Lord God,
We thank you for all the creatures who live on the earth;
for ants and antelopes,
for camels and crocodiles;
for llamas and leopards;
for zebras and zoos.
Help us to care for all animals,
and especially those for whom we are responsible. Amen.

➡️ *RE*
Find out about the work of Friends of the Earth (see Useful Addresses). Create prayers based on the theme of 'Animals'.

English
KS1: Find out about groups who care for animals or birds (e.g., RSPCA, Blue Cross, RSPB) and encourage pupils to talk about their work in groups.

   KS2: Consider this quote by Chief Seattle, written in 1854: 'This we know: The earth does not belong to us, we belong to the earth. This we know: All things are connected like the blood which unites one family . . . All things are connected. Whatever befalls the earth befalls the children of the earth. We did not weave the web of life; we are merely a strand in it. Whatever we do to the web, we do to ourselves!' Discuss the quotation and create poetry or drama using these words as a catalyst.

Science
Investigate what birds and animals use the school grounds. Collect evidence of footprints (by drawings, photographs, or plaster-casts) and identify the relevant birds or animals. Discover what birds eat, and make a 'fat ball' containing suitable foods (e.g., place nuts, seeds, etc. in a yoghurt carton, add melted fat and a piece of string to act as a hanger, then leave to set). If desired, create a display to encourage others to ask questions and investigate, and place it in an appropriate place.

IT
Keep a record of the birds and animals that use the school grounds, over a given period.

Art
Sketch pictures of the birds found in the school grounds.

SPEAKING

The ability to speak to one another is one that we often take for granted, but without it our lives would be very different. This week's assemblies explore speaking to other people and to God, but they also look at failing to speak—at those times when we should have spoken.

Speaking together (school or class assembly)

People meet together for all kinds of reasons—some good and some bad reasons. They might meet together to sing, to hold a meeting to discuss something important, to put out a fire, or to dance at a disco. But sometimes people also get together to cause riots, or to fight a war. One of the most important things we can all do is to meet in order to speak 'as one voice', that is, in order to change something.

Draw the inside of a house on a board, with bedrooms, a kitchen and one living room. Outside the house draw a small garden, and one medium-sized field. Then divide the pupils into a number of small groups. Each group is to be composed of certain animals or people. For example:

Groups:

1. Horses
2. Pet hamsters
3. Cats
4. Dogs
5. Children.

Tell each group that they belong to a farmer who lives on a small farm, in his farmhouse. Then get each group to decide exactly what they need in order to live a *good life* on the farm. For example:

1. Horses need:

    space to run (e.g., a meadow)
    somewhere warm to sleep (e.g., a barn)

food (e.g., hay or grass)
water
grooming.

2. Hamsters need:

a cage for safety (e.g., from the cats, dogs, humans and horses!)
water
food
exercise.

Make sure that there are some overlaps: for example, if the cats have the run of the house, what about the dogs, or a child who is allergic to cats? Or, if the horses use the field, what about exercising the dogs and the children? Allow pupils to be as selfish as possible, initially.

When each group has identified all their needs, ask them how they are going to solve their difficulties, and establish sensible rules for co-existence on the farm so that all the animals and children are fairly treated.

Alternatively, in a classroom assembly with younger children, allow each pupil to choose what area of activity they would like to work on during the day (e.g., home corner, jig-saws, sand or water play), and encourage them to work together to decide how they can do this so that everyone gets treated fairly. Create a timetable based on their suggestions.

Talk about trades unions and why they were formed ('a group of people often doing the same job may get together to try and improve their working conditions'). Comment on the standard of living that many people had in the nineteenth century, the way that children as young as seven and eight worked down mines for many hours at a time, often in darkness; or talk about those who climbed the chimneys to keep them clean. In the nineteenth century, men and women began to see that if they went to their employers and spoke together, it might be possible to change the way they worked and the money they earned.

When we get together and speak with one voice ('rather than fight') we can make changes—not just in our own country, but in other parts of the world. For instance, we can choose to stand up for others by demanding that large companies trade fairly so that those who grow coffee beans, or tea plants, receive a fair amount of money for their work. We can also speak in another way: we can choose who we want to run our local government and our national government. If enough people care about something then things can be changed.

When we tried to make some rules for our farm it was difficult, because we all wanted the best for ourselves. But finally we did agree what we should do—we listened to one another and thought about each other. We need to try and do this as much as possible in everything that we do.

 In these two stories of Paul and Barnabas, and of Jesus before Pilate, we see how people can be stirred up to do either good or evil. Acts 14.1–3 and Luke 23.13–21:

Acts 14.1–3:

Paul and Barnabas went to the synagogue (in Iconium) and spoke in such a way that a great number of Jews and Gentiles became believers. But the Jews who would not believe stirred up the Gentiles and turned them against the believers. The apostles stayed there for a long time, speaking boldly about the Lord, who proved that their message about his grace was true by giving them the power to perform miracles and wonders.

Luke 23.13–21:

Pilate called together the chief priests, the leaders, and the people, and said to them, 'You brought this man to me and said that he was misleading the people. Now, I have examined him here in your presence, and I have not found him guilty of any of the crimes you accuse him of . . . There is nothing this man has done to deserve death. So I will have him whipped and let him go.'

The whole crowd cried out, 'Kill him! Set Barabbas free for us!' (Barabbas had been put in prison for a riot that had taken place in the city, and for murder.)

Pilate wanted to set Jesus free, so he appealed to the crowd again. But they shouted back, 'Crucify him! Crucify him!'

 'Join with us to sing God's praises' (*BBC Complete Come and Praise* 30)
'O Praise ye the Lord!' (*BBC Complete Come and Praise* 37)

Lord God,
Help us to listen to one another,
and to think about one another,
especially when we have to make decisions.

Help us to work together for those
who are poor, or sick, or oppressed,
so that this world may be a happier place
for all people to live. Amen.

History
KS1: As part of a study of the everyday life of men, women and children in the past (perhaps of those in your locality), look at working conditions and at the differences that trades unions made to their lives. KS2: As part of a study of Victorian Britain, or Britain since 1930, or of local history, look at the life of those who worked in one or more industries, and at the changes made by the coming of the trades unions.

RE
KS1: Make a study of the early Church (see Acts 2), of their lifestyle, and of the number of converts. KS2: Make a study of the early Church, exploring the spread of Christianity from Jerusalem to the whole of the Middle East. How did the early churches become established, and what part did persecution play in Christianity's rapid spread?

English
KS1: Allow pupils to make decisions about their classroom, or the way in which they might work, encouraging them to listen to one another and make collective decisions. KS2: Create a newspaper for a trades union, many of whose members are about to be made redundant.

Music
Pupils could be taught a new song (unison), with the emphasis on singing and breathing together as one. KS2: Learn a round, or two-part song, with the emphasis on singing separate parts that combine as one harmonious whole.

PE
Explore mood and feeling in a dance, and learn a country dance where all have to work together as a whole. Alternatively, try maypole dancing.

Using our voice (class assembly)

We use our voices all day. We shout, talk, whisper, cajole and argue. From the moment we open our eyes our voices are in use. This assembly helps pupils and staff to concentrate on what we say when we use our voice, and to thank God for the marvel of speech.

Group pupils in twos, and ask them to think back over the conversations they have had during the last 24 hours. Who have they talked to (e.g., Mum, Dad, friends, brothers and sisters)? How many *kind* and helpful things have they said, and to whom did they say them? Be honest! KS2 children might like to write the list down.

Then in silence encourage them to think of those things they have said that were *unkind* and unhelpful in the last 24 hours. To whom did they say them? This list should not be written down.

The Book of Proverbs in the Old Testament contains practical sayings about the way we should behave in ordinary life. This book has quite a lot to say about the way in which we should speak to other people.

A good man's words are like pure silver; a wicked man's ideas are worthless. (Proverbs 10.20)

It is foolish to speak scornfully of others. If you are sensible, you will keep quiet. No one who gossips can be trusted with a secret, but you can put confidence in someone who is trustworthy. (Proverbs 11.12–13)

A gentle answer quietens anger, but a harsh one stirs it up. (Proverbs 15.1)

Our voices are very precious. Our voices can speak words of love ('to a baby'); words of encouragement ('to a child who is scared, or to someone who is running a race'); words of direction ('say, to the bus station'); and words of inspiration ('like a famous leader or preacher').

Unfortunately, our voices can also speak words of anger and hatred. We can say unkind things to friends and classmates, or to members of our family, and we can cause arguments or make others angry.

Perhaps the most important thing we can do is to think about what we're going to say, before we speak. Maybe then we wouldn't say things we wished unsaid later.

Lord God,
We thank you for our voices.
Help us to remember that we can use speech
to help other people,
to show them kindness and offer them hope.
Help us to think before we speak so that
we do not upset others or hurt them. Amen.

Science
KS2: Find out about the human voice. What parts of the body are used to produce our voice? Look at the way that singers or actors train their voices (e.g., the importance of posture, the way that certain things like chocolate, cigarettes and poor air quality are not ideal for the voice). NB The boys and girls who sing in most cathedral choirs are usually forbidden to eat chocolate before they sing!

Design Technology
KS1: Design and create a number of 'telephones' using any of the following items: plastic pots of different sizes and shapes, string, wool and wire. Vary the length of string/wool/wire. Which 'telephones' work the best? Encourage pupils to make suggestions as to why such a telephone works better than another.

English
Find out about different accents that people use (e.g. what parts of the country have strong accents; is there a 'normal' accent; which accents are difficult to understand and why?). If possible read *Ee by gum, Lord* by Arnold Kellett, or listen to a recording of this, the Bible in broad Yorkshire.

Music
Explore the flexibility of the singing voice: how high and how low pupils can sing (does the gender of the pupil make a difference?); look at speed and tempo; explore how long pupils can hold a note; and then listen to a singer with an unusual musical range. Finally, learn a new piece of music. Constantly express amazement at what the human voice can achieve.

RE
Learn one or more of the quotations from Proverbs. Listen to a recording of a section of the Bible by a noted actor. Alternatively, prepare a number of short readings from the Bible using the *Dramatised Bible*.

Speaking up for others (school assembly)

Often it does not occur to us to speak up for other people, or else we do not like to stand up for someone else, perhaps feeling it isn't our business. This assembly looks at what can happen when we really care about other people.

Tell the story of the early days of Amnesty International.
   In 1961 a British lawyer, Peter Benenson, wrote an article in a newspaper asking people to help free many thousands of men and women who were in prison. The men and women he wanted to be released from

AMNESTY
INTERNATIONAL
UNITED KINGDOM

prison had not been put into prison because they had done anything wrong. They were in prison because their political or religious beliefs differed from those who ran their country.

Peter Benenson argued that there were thousands of such people who had been thrown into prison and tortured for their beliefs: people who had been in prison for many years; people who had simply disappeared.

Immediately after the article appeared in the newspaper, many people contacted Peter Benenson, and Amnesty International was born. Now, many years later, Amnesty is a world-wide human rights movement. It has over 1.1 million members who work to release prisoners of conscience (that is 'those imprisoned for their beliefs, colour, gender, language or religion'), and to help them get fair trials. Amnesty has worked hard to get rid of the death penalty and to stop prisoners being tortured. It has also opposed the 'disappearances' that go on in many countries.

Its members often work in many small ways. Since its beginning in 1961 it has investigated more than 43,500 cases. Much of the work involves writing to governments and to prisoners themselves. One prisoner wrote:

> When the first two hundred letters came, the guards gave me back my clothes. Then the next two hundred letters came and the prison director came to see me . . . The letters kept coming and coming: three thousand of them. The President was informed. The letters still kept arriving and the President called the prison and told them to let me go. (Letter from a former prisoner of conscience from the Dominican Republic)

The work of Amnesty International goes on across the whole world, wherever men and women are imprisoned unjustly.

The story from the Bible today is about a city that was so wicked that God wanted to destroy it. But Abraham argued with God that he should not destroy everyone in the city in case he killed those people who were good. He spoke up for the people so strongly that God listened, as we shall hear. Genesis 18:20–33:

> Then the Lord said to Abraham, 'There are terrible accusations against Sodom and Gomorrah, and their sin is very great. I must go down to find out whether or not the accusations which I have heard are true.'. . .
> Abraham approached the Lord and asked, 'Are you really going to destroy the innocent with the guilty? If there are fifty innocent people in the city, will you destroy the whole city? Won't you spare it in order to

save the fifty? Surely you won't kill the innocent with the guilty. That's impossible! You can't do that. If you did, the innocent would be punished along with the guilty. That is impossible. The judge of all the earth has to act justly.'

The Lord answered, 'If I find fifty innocent people in Sodom, I will spare the whole city for their sake.'

Abraham spoke again: 'Please forgive my boldness in continuing to speak to you, Lord, I am only a man and have no right to say anything. But perhaps there will be only forty-five innocent people instead of fifty. Will you destroy the whole city because there are five too few?'

The Lord answered, 'I will not destroy the city if I find forty-five innocent people.'

Abraham spoke again: 'Perhaps there will be only forty.'

He replied, 'I will not destroy it if there are forty.'

Abraham said, 'Please don't be angry, Lord, but I must speak again. What if there are only thirty?'

He said, 'I will not do it if I find thirty.'

Abraham said, 'Please forgive my boldness in continuing to speak to you, Lord. Suppose that only twenty are found?'

He said, 'I will not destroy the city if I find twenty.'

Abraham said, 'Please don't be angry, Lord, and I will speak just once more. What if only ten are found?'

He said, 'I will not destroy it if there are ten.' After he had finished speaking with Abraham, the Lord went away, and Abraham returned home.

As we can see from the story of Amnesty International, when someone cares about others and speaks (or, in the case of Amnesty International, writes about them), things begin to change. And, when enough people speak up, governments and courts listen. When we speak up for other people we can change our society: we can bring justice to people, make prisoners free, and change laws.

Words can sometimes be more effective than fighting. We don't need to fight to help others, we can speak for them, and if enough of us care then changes will be made.

However, we need to be brave to stand up for other people. Abraham needed to be brave to stand up to God not once, but a number of times. But he cared so much for the *good* people of Sodom and Gomorrah that he continued to ask God to care for them. We too need to be brave when we stand up for others, especially when others are against us.

'You gotta have love in your heart' (*BBC Complete Come and Praise* 87)

'A still small voice in the heart of the city' (*BBC Complete Come and Praise* 96)

 Write a litany on the lines of the following:

Leader: Lord God, help us to speak for others when they need our help. Lord, hear us.

All: Lord, hear us.

Leader: Lord God, help us to be brave when we have to stand up for other people. Lord, hear us. . . .

 English
KS1: Read a book on bullying (e.g., *Jimmy Woods and the Big Bad Wolf* by Mick Gower, or *Ombibomulator* by Dick King-Smith). KS2: Contact local members of Amnesty International and find out more about their work. Write specimen letters regarding prisoners, and create a display (or choose to send the letters).

RE
KS1: Talk about bullying and standing up for other children in school. KS2: Find out what happened to the people of Sodom and Gomorrah by reading the rest of the story in Genesis 19.1–2a, 12–29, or talk about bullying in school and create an anti-bullying charter.

History
As part of the study unit on Victorian Britain find out about a social reformer who stood up for ordinary men and women and tried to change society (e.g., Lord Shaftesbury, Florence Nightingale, Robert Raikes).

Design Technology/IT
Design a questionnaire, after discussion, to discover the extent of bullying in your school. Test it on a small number of pupils, make suggestions about how to proceed, and modify the questionnaire as appropriate. Store the information concerning the anti-bullying

---

charter on computer, retrieve, process and display the information as appropriate. Use the information to create an anti-bullying charter (see *RE* above), and then feed information to the school governors who are ultimately responsible for discipline in the school.

Speaking to God (class assembly)

We speak to each other and to our friends each day, but speaking to God can be difficult. This assembly looks at how we might speak to God.

 In pairs, ask pupils to talk about what they would like to say to, or ask, God (e.g., Why did you make the world? Why do people suffer? Please look after my Gran who is ill.)

Encourage the class to listen to each other's questions, requests and comments. (If there are two or three subjects that come up consistently, look at these later, perhaps in RE.)

If desired, and if time permits, begin to look at some of the subjects that come up. (A book that will help with the answers is *Will My Rabbit Go to Heaven?* by Jeremie Hughes.)

 Some people who constantly turned to God, not just to ask his help but also to complain, were the writers of the psalms. In the reading today we see a number of different people and their conversations with God.

Someone asking God for help—Psalm 59.1–2:

> Save me from my enemies, my God;
> protect me from those who attack me!
> Save me from those evil men;
> rescue me from those murderers.

Praising God—Psalm 92.1–2:

> How good it is to give thanks to you, O Lord,
> to sing in your honour, O Most High God,
> to proclaim your constant love every morning
> and your faithfulness every night.

We can talk to God in the same way that we talk to the people around us. We don't need to use special language, we can talk to him just as we talk to our friends. We can thank God for what he has done for us; we can ask him to help us; we can tell him how great he is; we can even moan at him.

Sometimes we might want to find somewhere quiet to talk to God, but at other times we can just send him a quick thought in the middle of whatever we are doing—like 'Help, God!' (These are called arrow prayers!) But we must not forget to keep talking to God.

 Encourage the pupils to use these questions to God as the starting-point for some silent prayer, and end by asking God to 'Hear our prayer'. Alternatively, create a prayer:

Leader: Lord God, we thank you today for all the things that you have given us . . . (allow pupils to add the things they wish to thank God for, in silence)

Leader: Lord God, we ask you to forgive us for the things we have done wrong . . .

Leader: Lord God, we ask you to help those people of whom we are thinking . . .

Leader: Lord God, hear our prayer this day. Amen.

RE
Explore different prayer postures (e.g., standing with hands upraised; kneeling with heads bowed, eyes closed and hands together; laying face down; hands held on lap but 'face' up). When and where might they be used and by whom? Talk about praying when we are doing other things (e.g., sitting on a bus or in a car, painting, singing).

English
Create poems or prayers to God. Create a prayerful atmosphere as the pupils carry out this task by playing suitable quiet music. Explain that the writing in itself can be a prayer.

Art
Create borders suitable to display the poems or prayers to God (see *English*), using a new media.

Music
Create some quiet music that could help people pray.

Note: The prayers, art and music, could all be used in another assembly.

Speaking to others (school assembly)

God expects his people to speak to others—to tell them the good news about his love for his people. In the Bible there are many people who were sent out by God to do his work.

Over the past few hundred years many men and women have travelled across the world to tell people about God. Often they did not speak the language of the people to whom they were going, and they were forced to put up with all kinds of hardships. Many died for their beliefs.

These people were called missionaries. They often started schools or hospitals to help local people, and taught them all kinds of skills. Of course, they also taught many children and adults about Christianity.

Tell the story of the oldest missionary society in the world, the story of SPCK—a missionary society that did not provide people, but books and education, to teach the people about God.

The Society for Promoting Christian Knowledge, or SPCK as it is usually known, was started 300 years ago. On 8 March 1698, five men met in

Lincolns Inn, London. The leader was the Rev. Thomas Bray, and the other men were Lord Guildford, Sir Humphrey Mackworth, Colonel Maynard Colchester and Serjeant Hook, at whose house they first met.

These five men were worried that many people in England and abroad (especially in places like America) were not being taught the Christian faith. Children did not have to attend school, and most adults could not read or write. Indeed, most children started to work when they were very young and did not have time to attend school. The only place that people could learn about God was at church on Sunday.

Thomas Bray and the other four men drew up plans to 'promote Religion and Learning in the Plantations abroad and to propagate Christian Knowledge at home'. In the first two years of the Society, the five men set about planning to set up charity schools to teach poor children. Hundreds of primary schools in England were to be started with money from SPCK. Children were to be educated free of charge.

By 1700 the Society had also begun publishing books to go out to churches overseas, and was planning to publish books in different languages, not just in English. The first of these were printed in Welsh and in Dutch, and by 1720 they were printing copies of the New Testament and the Psalter in Arabic. To pay for all this work special appeals were held.

Over the next century the Society continued to publish Bibles, hymn books, psalters and prayer books in many different kinds of languages, and to send them out all over the world. In 1811 it set up the National Society to take over the work of building new schools. In 1832 the Society began to publish other good educational books, especially children's books, and in 1836 it opened its first bookshop in London.

Over 300 years the work of SPCK has flourished, and it still goes on today. It runs over thirty bookshops in England, selling all kinds of Christian books and goods, from Bibles to candles, from books on back pain to crosses. Its publishing house continues to publish books on many subjects, from prayer books to assembly books (like this one), which are sold across the world. Thousands of books are still published in hundreds of different languages, though many are now published by sister organizations from places like America, Australia and India. The work of raising money to build libraries and training colleges; to publish books in languages that the people can understand; and to provide books for men and women who are training to be readers or priests, still continues. Each year SPCK gives away nearly half a million pounds for this very important work.

Although we call SPCK a missionary society we can see that it did not send missionaries out to convert people to Christianity; instead it sent out books and pamphlets to teach the people what it meant to be a Christian, and it provided hymn books and prayer books for the people to worship God in their own language.

We may not be called to go out and work in other countries of the world to tell the people about God, or like SPCK to provide books and money to teach people about God. But there are many people who still do. Sometimes they go and help to build churches, or teach in schools, or nurse in local hospitals.

Talk about others who tell people about God: the local vicar or minister (name them) who is called to tell people about God (explain how: e.g., through sermons, talks, baptism or confirmation classes); some churches (or the diocese) have 'evangelists' or 'missioners'—men and women set aside to do the special work of telling people about God and about his son, Jesus.

All those who are baptized (or 'christened') should always be ready to tell others about God.

Jesus tells his disciples what will happen to them if they obey his command to take God's words and to speak to the people. He also tells them that they should not worry what they should say if they are arrested and taken to court. Matthew 10.16–20:

'Listen! I am sending you out just like sheep to a pack of wolves. You must be as cautious as snakes and as gentle as doves. Watch out, for there will be men who will arrest you and take you to court, and they will whip you in the synagogues. For my sake you will be brought to trial before rulers and kings, to tell the Good News to them and to the Gentiles. When they bring you to trial, do not worry about what you are going to say or how you will say it; when the time comes, you will be given what you are going to say. For the words you will speak will not be yours; they will come from the Spirit of your Father speaking through you.'

 'In Christ there is no east or west' (BBC *Complete Come and Praise* 66)

'The ink is black, the page is white' (BBC *Complete Come and Praise* 67)

101

Lord God,
We thank you that there are people brave enough to tell others about you.
Help us to have the courage to tell others
of the things we believe in.
And help us to listen to those who talk about you
and all you have done for us. Amen.

 RE
Find out about the work of some missionaries (e.g., those working for SAMS or CMS—see Useful Addresses).

History
KS1: Look at the life of any saint called to take the news about God to another community or country. This could be someone who lived in the past in the locality (e.g., those in the north of England or in Scotland might like to look at St Columba or St Aidan). KS2: As part of the study unit Victorian Britain explore the work of those who wanted to make Christianity available to the masses in Britain (e.g., Robert Raikes of Gloucester who set up the first Sunday School for poor children).

English
In twos, encourage pupils to tell each other about things which are important to them (e.g., hobbies, family, animals, clubs). Give pupils time to prepare what they will say, and encourage good habits of listening by ensuring that pupils understand they will all have time to talk. Give them vocabulary that might be helpful (special, important, etc.). Afterwards talk about how easy or difficult it is to speak about things which are very important to us. Explore whether it is as easy to speak about matters of faith in this way.

IT
Ask a local minister to come in to school and explore with them in what ways, other than speech, they tell people about God (e.g. posters, magazines, Internet). If the school has access to the Internet look up a web-site devoted to a Christian organization.

RELATIONSHIPS

Throughout our life we have to be able to get on with people. We rarely live completely on our own, and even then we have neighbours or family that we see from time to time. To be human is to live in a community with other people, and we have to learn how to live together in harmony. This week we spend time looking at our relationships with other people, and how we can help to improve them.

Parents (school or class assembly)

One of the closest relationships that most of us have is with our parents or guardians. Today this may be with natural parents or with step-parents. Often our relationship is close and loving, but even a good relationship can suffer difficulties. Jesus reminds us that God is the ultimate good parent.

 Take an object into the assembly that reminds you of one of your parents. Alternatively, ask two or three members of staff, or some parents or grandparents, to bring in suitable objects. Show the object to pupils and share your memories with them. If possible look at objects which show different aspects of parental love (caring, feeding, clothing, loving, etc.).

Alternatively, for a class assembly, ask pupils to talk about the ways in which their parents or guardians care for them. Write these up on a board and draw or place a picture alongside to demonstrate each aspect.

Jesus taught us to speak to God as we would speak to our father (or mother), and to ask him for help. Luke 11.1–4:

One day Jesus was praying in a certain place. When he had finished, one of his disciples said to him, 'Lord, teach us to pray, just as John taught his disciples.'

Jesus said to them, 'When you pray, say this:

Father:
May your holy name be honoured;

103

may your Kingdom come.
Give us day by day the food we need.
Forgive us our sins,
for we forgive everyone who does us wrong.
And do not bring us to hard testing.'

 God cares for us a parent cares for their child. He loves us as a *good* father loves his child.

(*Note*: Emphasize the word *good*. Some parents may not be good parents, and there may be pupils present in the assembly who do not know a loving and stable home, but the principle is still the same, that God loves us like a good parent.)

As we have seen, a good parent takes care of us from the time we are born. They feed us, clothe us and love us. When we are horrible, they love us; when we are unkind they love us; when we are ill they love us.

God is just like this to us, his children. No matter what we are like, God loves us.

 Use the pictures or objects as a basis for prayer, to say thank you to God, and to ask his loving care for those who do not have good relationships with their parents or guardians.

 'Fill your hearts with joy' (*BBC Complete Come and Praise 9*)

History
In the study unit on Britain since 1930 look at parenting during World War Two—at evacuation, at one-parent families with fathers away at war, at the role of grandparents at this time, etc.

Science
KS1: Find out about babies: their dependency, food, at what stages they can smile, cry, frown, pick up items, etc. KS2: Look at growth and reproduction in humans and at the main stages of the human life-cycle with an emphasis on parenting.

English

KS2: Write letters from a parent to a child away from home in a dangerous situation (e.g., at war, or in a hostage situation). Alternatively, create articles for a newspaper on 'Parents'—these could be stories or poems about good or bad parents. Read *Other Bells For Us to Ring* by Robert Cormier, the story of a girl searching for her father in wartime.

RE

Look at the story of Moses as a baby (Exodus 2.1–10), and explore how his mother might have felt at placing him in the bulrushes and then at having him brought up by Pharaoh's daughter. Alternatively explore the phrase 'Parents/Step-parents are . . . !' Be sensitive to answers and help pupils to look at situations from their parents' point of view.

Art

Look at famous pictures of mothers and babies. These will often be religious, but could include more modern examples. Explore changes in style. KS1: Look at early photographs of themselves with their mothers. How different are these from the pictures already explored? KS2: Ask a mother and her baby to act as a model and encourage pupils to draw or paint their own pictures.

Brothers and sisters (class assembly)

Most of us have brothers and sisters (and for those who haven't there are probably other close relatives like cousins, or step-brothers and -sisters) with whom we live most, or some, of the time. Getting on with them can be very difficult. We can feel jealous of them, or find their behaviour irritating. Whatever the reason, there are times when we have to work hard to get on with them. This assembly looks at how we can improve things.

 Give each pupil a piece of paper. Older pupils might like to draw a vertical scale on the paper from 0 at the bottom to 10 at the top.
Ask the class to think about a brother or sister (or cousin, or step-

brother or -sister) with whom they have some problems, or have had problems in the past (these could be a younger child who invades their bedroom or destroys their work; an older child who laughs, teases or hits them; or a baby of whom they are jealous). Ask them to think about the other person for a moment—about the things they like and dislike about them. Then when they are ready they should draw a picture of this person. Depending on the size of the problems draw a small or large figure. (*Note*: If a child is really having difficulties with someone else in the family the picture should fill the whole paper.)

Encourage pupils to draw their pictures in silence, and then to share their thoughts with each other or with you, as is appropriate.

Everyone has trouble with members of their family at some time in their life. It is quite normal. However, we should always try to get on with each other, and sometimes this means we have to work hard at it. We have to stop ourselves 'winding people up', especially if we know they have a quick temper; we have to stop ourselves doing things that will deliberately upset them (for example, going into their bedrooms when we know they don't like it, or upsetting their games, or whatever it is we know they don't like); and we have to think of ways of doing things that will please them.

Because we know each other so well, it can be harder to live in peace with members of our family than it can be with our friends. But God wants us to try to live together happily, and we must try to find ways of living in peace.

St Paul reminds us that each of us needs to have love in our hearts. If we have love in our hearts then we will be the kind of people that God wants us to be. And with love in our hearts we will try to find ways of making our relationships with our brothers and sisters better. 1 Corinthians 13.1–3 (or 4):

> I may be able to speak the languages of men and even of angels, but if I have no love, my speech is no more than a noisy gong or a clanging bell. I may have all knowledge and understand all secrets; I may have all the faith needed to move mountains—but if I have no love, I am nothing. (verse 4: I may give away everything I have, and even give up my body to be burnt—but if I have no love, this does me no good.)

 Encourage pupils to look at their pictures, and in silence to ask God to help them get on better with the person whom they have drawn.

English
Read *Friends and Brothers* by Dick King-Smith to pupils, or *The Lark Who Had No Song* by Carolyn Nystrom. KS2: Read the story of The Prodigal Son (Luke 15.11–end) and discuss why the elder brother was so cross, and how the two brothers might have been reconciled.

RE
Explore further the problems that can occur in families between brothers, sisters and cousins. Talk about how pupils can deal with these, encouraging them to offer sensitive suggestions. Write down confessions, and be sure to dispose of these effectively.

Science
Continue the theme of relationships by exploring the relationship between opaque objects and shadows. Gather a number of objects, some translucent and some opaque, and encourage pupils to predict whether they will cause a shadow. Use the sun, or a torch if the day is dull, to test their predictions. Create shadows. What shapes can be made? What causes a shadow to be elongated, or squat?

Mathematics
KS1: Look at the language of relationships (e.g., 'bigger than', 'next to', 'before'). Alternatively, look at simple patterns and relationships and make related predictions about them. KS2: Look at relationships (e.g., 'multiple of', 'factor of', or 'symmetrical to').

Strangers (school assembly)

This week's assemblies have been looking at ways in which we can improve our relationships with different people, but today's assembly is a reminder that we have to be careful with people we don't know.

 Tell the story of Tom and the football game.

Tom was 9 years old. On a good day, he had red hair—under control. On a good day, he was Tom Best footballer extraordinaire. On a good day, he escaped trouble.

Unfortunately good days didn't happen very often. His red hair usually stood up like a question mark, and he always seemed to be in trouble—either with his mum, or with Mrs Stevens his teacher, or with someone! Not that Tom minded too much, as long as he had got his football.

Football was Tom's life. His mum said he ate, slept, thought and dreamt football. She said that if there wasn't football in his day, then he became like a zombie. Tom thought his Mum exaggerated a little, though he did agree that he played a lot of football.

Tom played for the school football 1st XI team every week, and he usually managed to score one or two goals. He met twice a week with the team for training, and every Saturday morning he turned out for the local football club, where he learnt new skills. His mum complained at the amount of washing she had to do, but Tom knew that she was proud of him, and she never failed to come and watch him play.

Tom's friends, Alex and Richard, also liked football. If they weren't playing it, then they were watching it. Newcastle was their team, and black and white their colours. In fact, if the school uniform hadn't been blue, they'd probably have worn black and white to school as well. Their rooms were black and white, they wore black jeans and white T-shirts, and even black and white socks and shoes. Tom's mum said it made her eyes feel funny always ironing black and white things!

Every Saturday Tom and his friends met outside the village shop sharp at 9 a.m. in the morning. It was the one morning they were never late, no matter what time they went to bed. Usually Richard was there first, but the other two joined him a moment or two afterwards. From there they went on to the village hall, and its three football pitches.

'Dribble, I said, Tom—not waddle!' shouted Mr Sharp, the football coach. 'What's the matter with you, boy?'

Tom pulled a face, and tried to concentrate on what his feet were doing. 'He knows that I'm doing my best—why can't he pick on someone else!'

'Shoot, Tom! Shoot, for goodness sake!' Mr Sharp flung his hands to his head. 'Come on, Tom. Wake up!'

Tom got control of the ball, but it was no good. Somehow his feet would not obey him. He knew why! He was tired. Mum and Dad had gone out late last night and the babysitter had let him stay up late.

'Bill! Come and take Tom's place!' shouted Mr Sharp, to a young boy standing on the touchline. 'Perhaps you can do better!'

Tom kicked the ground angrily. He knew it was his own fault, but it didn't help. Bill passed him, and smiled sympathetically. 'Sorry, Tom!' he said.

'It's all right! It's not your fault. It's all mine.' Tom clenched his fists, determined to go off without complaint.

He reached the touchline, and turned to watch the rest of the game, hardly knowing what he was seeing in his misery.

'Never mind, youngster!' said a soft voice near him. 'Better luck next time.'

Tom looked up at the man standing near him. 'Thanks!' he said.

'I've seen you here before, haven't I? You're the one that normally gets the goals, aren't you?' The man smiled at Tom, sympathetically.

Tom nodded. 'Yes! I've been lucky. But it was my own fault today.'

'Oh! I don't know. He was a bit hard on you, don't you think?' The tall man smiled at Tom, and held out his hand. 'My name is Andy, by the way.'

Tom shook hands with him. 'Mine's Tom,' he said.

'Well, now that we're friends, you'll have to tell me. Why was it your fault?'

'I was up too late last night, and I'm feeling tired,' he said, rather shame-facedly. 'Mum's always nagging me to get more sleep. I reckon she's right this time!'

Andy shook his head, laughing. 'Rubbish! Look at me, I never get to bed till late at night, but I'm still OK the next day. It must just be an unlucky day for you.'

Tom smiled back. 'Perhaps you're right,' he said, feeling much better already.

'What about coming for a can of cola, if they don't want you at the moment?' He pointed across the football pitches to the small cafe in the distance. 'You'll still be able to see the game from there.'

The idea was tempting. If they didn't want Tom on the pitch, well at least his new friend seemed to want him. He hesitated.

'Come on! What harm can it do? You can come back when they need you, after all.' Andy touched his arm.

'OK! But I don't want to be gone too long. Thanks,' he added, remembering his manners.

The man and the boy moved away, past the goal posts, and round the other pitches towards the small cafe, talking as they went. The cafe proved to be warm and at this time of the morning there was no one else in the place. Tom was enjoying himself. It wasn't often he had an adult interested in football willing to listen to him.

After a while, though, his attention began to wander towards the football pitch. 'I think I ought to get back,' he said finally. 'I might be needed!' He looked at Andy, a little apologetically.

Andy shrugged. 'OK! If that's what you want,' he said. 'But I thought we might go for a swim, or see a film, if you've nothing better to do.'

Tom looked at his friend, and frowned. 'Well, I'd love to, but I promised Mum I'd go home first, and, well, she'll worry if I don't.'

'Well, please yourself. It's no sweat off my nose! I've got to go, anyway.' Andy got up. 'Perhaps I'll see you, sometime!'

Tom felt awful, after all Andy had been pretty good to him. Perhaps he should go with him. It couldn't do any harm. He could always tell Mum afterwards.

'Tom! I think they need you on the pitch.' The voice came from the doorway.

'Mum!' Tom leapt across the room to hug his Mum. 'What are you doing here? I thought you couldn't make it, this morning?'

'Well, I managed to get away earlier than I thought. Mr Sharp wondered where you'd got to. He says they need you urgently.' She hugged him back.

Tom began to leave, keen to get back to the game, then he remembered his new friend. 'Mum, I want you to meet Andy. He's been smashing.'

Tom looked round the small room. Where had Andy gone? There was no one else in the room. He looked up at his mum, puzzled. 'Where's he gone, Mum?'

Mrs Holmes looked down at her small son. 'I think he's gone,' she said quietly. 'You see, he wasn't quite the nice man you thought.'

Tom frowned.

'He shouldn't have asked you to leave the football pitch. Mr Sharp was very worried because he didn't know where you'd gone.'

'But Andy was kind, and he listened to me,' protested Tom.

'I know, Tom. But we can't be sure about people we don't know—about people who are strangers. It's always better to say "No!" to strangers, even when they're very nice.'

'What about people I know?' he asked, as they walked across the field.

'Sometimes we have to say "No!" to people we know, as well. If you're not sure about something that an adult asks you to do, it's always best to say "No—I won't go with you." Or, "No! I won't do that." After all,' said his mother, laughing, 'you don't want to miss a game do you?'

'No way!' grinned Tom, as he raced across the field to join in the last few moments of the game.

'The Lord, the Lord' (*BBC Complete Come and Praise* 108)
'The King of Love' (*BBC Complete Come and Praise* 54)

 The book of Psalms gives us some good advice. Psalm 1.1–4:

Happy are those
who reject the advice of evil men
who do not follow the example of God.

Instead, they find joy in obeying the
Law of the Lord,
and they study it day and night.

They are like trees that grow beside a stream,
that bear fruit at the right time,
and whose leaves do not dry up.
They succeed in everything they do.

But evil men are not like this at all;
they are like straw that the wind blows away.

This week we have been looking at how we can get on better with members of our family and with our friends. But today we are looking at something a little different. In the story of Tom and his football we are reminded that we shouldn't talk to people we don't know.

Sometimes we meet people who seem very friendly, but if we don't know them (or if we do know them, but we're not sure that Mum would let us go with them) we should never go off with them as Tom did. Others who are looking after us would become very worried if we disappeared in this way. No matter how nice someone may seem, and whether they are a man or a woman, we must always say 'No!'

It doesn't matter if we seem rather rude by saying 'No!' A really nice man or woman would understand and not mind. This is the one time we don't have to worry about trying to get on with someone.

 Lord God,
Help us to be wise in the ways of the world—
aware that not everyone around us is as nice as they seem.
Keep us safe in all that we do,
and watch over us. Amen.

Science
Look at the hazards and risks associated with some current work, and establish a code of good practice with pupils, emphasizing health and safety aspects. Encourage pupils to think of ways to take action to avoid risks. Ask questions like 'What would the safest action be?' and 'How can we be sure that this is the safest way to act?'

RE
Gently explore the notion of 'private space' with pupils, and adult behaviour that is acceptable to them. For example: If we like to have our hair combed, who would we allow to do that? Whose hand might we hold? Who might give us a kiss? Encourage pupils to see that all this can be very acceptable in our families, but we would not wish to do this outside the family.

English
KS1: Look at what it might feel like to get lost. Have any pupils experienced this? Where would pupils go if they were lost in town, or the countryside? KS2: Look in detail at the story 'Tom and the football game'. Encourage groups of pupils to take the part of different characters in the story. How would each character feel, and what might they like to say to each other? For example, how did Mr Sharp feel when Tom walked off the pitch? What did Tom's mother feel when she turned up and couldn't see her son?

Art
Express feelings about being lost through colour or shape.

Friends (class assembly)

Friendships can last for many years, indeed for a lifetime. But pupils need to learn the importance of working on friendships if the relationships are to mature and grow.

 Before the assembly make name cards for each pupil.

During the assembly make fuzzies (i.e., coloured cotton wool balls with felt-tip pen faces marked on them). Explain that a fuzzy is a soft little creature. Fuzzies are always given to you by another person, and they make you feel warm and happy because they are such nice little creatures.

Then in groups of about 12 pupils (these could be divided by gender, or if the class is accustomed to engaging in 'circle time' then this group should be used), sit in circles (either on the floor or at a group of tables). Place the name cards in the middle, face down. In turn each pupil should pick up a card and read out the name of the person to whom it belongs. Some pupils may need help with this.

Finally, the pupil should give their fuzzy to the other child, and say something complimentary to them (e.g., 'I like your shoes!' or 'I like the way you're always happy!'). Continue until all the name cards are turned face up, encouraging pupils to find something nice to say about each person.

You might wish to look at what kinds of complimentary sayings could be used before the assembly.

Jesus taught us a very important commandment. Perhaps it is the most important instruction that he gave us. John 15.12–14:

'My commandment is this: love one another, just as I love you. The greatest love a person can have for his friends is to give his life for them. And you are my friends if you do what I command you.'

Jesus taught us to love one another. By this he meant we should think about other people as if we were thinking about ourselves. We should behave towards others as we want them to behave towards us.

113

Over the years we will have many friendships, but if we are to keep our friends then we need to think about them—what they would like, and how they feel.

As we have seen today, we can always find something nice to say about a person, if we think about it. Unfortunately, sometimes we forget to give other people compliments, although we may say something nice about them to another person. Sometimes we get into the habit of only complaining to others. Or perhaps we take our friends for granted.

We need to remember that everyone likes to feel wanted, and we need to get into the habit of looking for the good qualities in everyone we meet. If our friendships are to last for a long time ('If all the people in this class are to stay friends for many years') then we must work on making our friendships better.

 Encourage pupils to be silent for a moment and to think of their friends—of what they look like, of their good qualities, etc. In the silence, thank God for all that they mean to us.

RE
Read the story of the friendship between Jonathan and David and in particular how Jonathan protected David from his father, King Saul (1 Samuel 20). Explore the theme of *friendship*. What do pupils look for in a friend? What things should a friend not do? How long can friendships last? Can we be friends if we live a long way apart? Create some work perhaps involving pictures of their friends, and display.

History
Use the theme of Friends to look at a friendship associated with the period of history being studied.

Design Technology
Design and make a letterbox to be used in school, either at Christmas to send letters to Santa Claus, or as part of a Post Office corner in the KS1 classroom.

Optional: Add a flap to the letterbox 'to keep out bad weather', and a means for the 'postman' to open the box to take out the letters.

English
KS2: Contact another school at some distance and set up a system of pen-friends for pupils. Encourage them to write and find out about each other.

God (school assembly)

Pupils should be helped to see that God, too, can be a friend. As they can turn to their friends for help and companionship, so they can turn to God, for he also loves us.

 Produce a short sketch, on the lines of the following, to demonstrate some aspects of friendship.

Cast: The Narrator (the teacher)
Vicky
6 pupils (boys and girls)

The sketch starts with the Narrator and Vicky out front. As the other children are named they should join Vicky. They might want to shake hands, or in some other more informal way indicate their friendship with Vicky. Vicky gives each of them a card, No. 1 to the first friend, No. 2 to the second and so on.

The Narrator introduces Vicky: Vicky is a girl who has lots of friends. Look at her friends, starting with her best friend, and going on to her second-best friend, etc. Introduce the friends (and include the following information):

Sam: Lives next door to Vicky, and they see each other every day. They watch television, talk, and play on the computer together. (No. 1)

Claire: Vicky's best friend *at school*. They see each other every day, sit next to each other in most lessons, and spend hours talking together at school, though as Claire lives a long way away they don't meet at weekends or in the holidays. (No. 2)

Alex: Vicky's cousin, who lives a few miles away. They see each other when their families get together, and ring each other up occasionally. (No. 3)

Susan: A friend that Vicky sees each Saturday at swimming, where they have a drink and talk each week. (No. 4)

George: Lived next door to Vicky before she moved away. They sometimes ring each other up. (No. 5)

Toni: A cousin who lives in ____ (name a town hundreds of miles away). They meet once a year at Christmas. (No. 6)

Add that Vicky has one more friend—God.

Explore with the pupils why it might be that the friends are in this order. What helps to cement the friendships (e.g., being together, talking to each other)?

Our closest friends are usually those people we see regularly (though not always!). We like to spend time with them, doing things together and getting to know them.

When we make God one of our friends we also want to talk to him (through prayer), we want to spend time with him (in worship), and we want to get to know him (by reading the Bible), just as we do with all our other friends. We may not be able to see him, but we can be with him daily.

Many thousands of years ago God spoke to the prophet Hosea. In our reading he uses picture language to try and explain to Hosea how much he loves the people of Israel. Hosea 11.1–4:

When Israel was a child, I loved him
and called him out of Egypt as my son.
But the more I called to him,
the more he turned away from me.
My people sacrificed to Baal;
they burnt incense to idols.
Yet I was the one who taught Israel to walk.
I took my people up in my arms,
but they did not acknowledge that I took care of them.
I drew them to me with affection and love.
I picked them up and held them to my cheek;
I bent down to them and fed them.

Use a large crucifix or picture of the crucifixion as an aid to 'eyes open' prayer.

Lord God,
You care for us as our closest friend:
even when we ignore or hurt you
you are still there for us;
even when we forget or anger you
you are still there for us.
Help us to get to know you better,
by learning more about you,
and by listening to your still small voice in our hearts. Amen.

 'God in his love' (*BBC Complete Come and Praise* 76)
'The King of Love' (*BBC Complete Come and Praise* 54)

RE
Draw pictures of God: 'What shape is God to you?' 'What colour is God to you?' etc. Talk about God, perhaps in small groups, but carry this out, if possible, after the pupils have drawn their pictures. Close with a reassuring story or image of God (e.g., the story of The Lost Sheep: Matthew 18.12–14).

Science
As part of work on green plants as organisms explore the diversity, number, colour and intricacy of flowering plants. Emphasize that we live in an amazing world created by God (KS2: 'ruled by natural selection, but initiated by God').

Art
Continue the exploration of flowering plants and create collage work, or sketch plants.

Mathematics
Using flowers, dissect them to discover how many mathematical shapes and patterns can be identified. Draw the shapes, name and display them.

Music

Learn a new hymn or song about God. Alternatively, listen to a famous anthem about God.

Week 9

CHANGE

We all experience change in our lives. From the moment we are born we begin to grow physically and our bodies change. We also experience change in other ways. Our attitudes change as we grow and mature, and if we move away from home we make new friends. Change is common to all human beings, though few of us really like change. We prefer to stay with the comfortable and the familiar. This week's assemblies look at the subject of change from a number of different viewpoints.

Changing viewpoint (school assembly)

All of us make decisions about things in our life. We know what we like, and what we believe. However, we need to be encouraged to re-examine these occasionally, and if necessary to change our viewpoint.

Using a photocopying machine, enlarge a picture of a well-known object (e.g., a comb, an ear-ring, a watch). The final magnification should concentrate on one aspect of the object only. Ideally the picture should be magnified sufficiently so that it is very difficult to identify the object. If desired, photocopy more than one object.

Ask pupils to try and identify the picture, and give clues if necessary. Finally, give them the answers and show them the original picture.

Alternatively, talk about pictures made on computers that use a series of dots or crosses. Up close they do not look like a picture, but when held further away the picture can be seen; or the view from two windows where one window shows an ugly view, but in the other the view is beautiful.

Comment on how difficult it was to guess the items concerned. Refer to any wild guesses, or to those who finally guessed correctly. Add that looking at objects in this way is a little like trying to look at a picture when we are too far away. Things don't seem quite right, and it is very hard to see at what we are looking.

What we see depends on where we are standing (or out of which window we look), or on how close we are looking at the view. Sometimes in our life we need to move and see things in a different way. When we look at things differently we may find out different things about ourselves, and about our friends and relations.

Our reading today is about someone who had to look at things differently, and to change his mind.

◆ Zechariah was a priest in the Temple at Jerusalem. He and his wife had no children, and they were both old. So, when an angel came to tell him that they would shortly have a son, Zechariah did not believe him. However, he was forced to change his mind. Luke 1.5–8, 11–20, 57–64:

> During the time when Herod was king of Judaea, there was a priest named Zechariah, who belonged to the priestly order of Abijah. His wife's name was Elizabeth; she also belonged to a priestly family. They both lived good lives in God's sight and obeyed fully all the Lord's laws, and commands. They had no children because Elizabeth could not have any, and she and Zechariah were both very old.
>
> One day Zechariah was doing his work as a priest in the Temple . . . An angel of the Lord appeared to him, standing on the right of the altar where the incense was burnt. When Zechariah saw him, he was alarmed and felt afraid. But the angel said to him, 'Don't be afraid, Zechariah! God has heard your prayer, and your wife Elizabeth will bear you a son. You are to name him John. How glad and happy you will be, and how happy many others will be when he is born! He will be a great man in the Lord's sight. He must not drink any wine or strong drink. From his very birth he will be filled with the Holy Spirit, and he will bring back many of the people of Israel to the Lord their God . . . '
>
> Zechariah said to the angel, 'How shall I know if this is so? I am an old man, and my wife is old also.'
>
> 'I am Gabriel,' the angel answered. 'I stand in the presence of God, who sent me to speak to you and tell you this good news. But you have not believed my message, which will come true at the right time. Because you have not believed, you will be unable to speak; you will remain silent until the day my promise to you comes true.' . . .
>
> The time came for Elizabeth to have her baby, and she gave birth to a son. Her neighbours and relatives heard how wonderfully good the Lord had been to her, and they all rejoiced with her.
>
> When the baby was a week old, they came to circumcise him, and they were going to name him Zechariah, after his father. But his mother said, 'No! His name is to be John.'

They said to her, 'But you have no relatives with that name!' Then they made signs to his father, asking him what name he would like the boy to have.

Zechariah asked for a writing tablet and wrote, 'His name is John.' How surprised they all were! At that moment Zechariah was able to speak again, and he started praising God.

'Break out' (*BBC Complete Come and Praise* 91)
'A still small voice' (*BBC Complete Come and Praise* 96)

Create a litany on the lines of the following:

Leader: Lord God,
           We are grateful that you have given us minds to think.
    All: We thank you, Lord.
Leader: We are grateful that you have made us to grow and change.
    All: We thank you, Lord.
Leader: We are grateful that you encourage us to think for ourselves...

English
Discuss what it feels like to 'change your mind'. Look at examples like: choosing a cake, going to the cinema or the swimming pool, what to give someone for a Christmas present, etc. In small groups produce some role-play on 'Changing my mind'. Or read *The Frightful Food Feud* by Brian Sibley, and discuss.

RE
Invite a speaker to come in who has changed their mind. This could be someone who has recently become a Christian; someone who has changed denominations; or perhaps a person who has recently changed their mind about the career or course they were going to do. Explore what emotions they went through, the difficulties of deciding, and how they now feel about the change.

Mathematics
KS1: Look at change in mathematics: work on numerals and symbols (e.g., change plus (+) symbols to minus (−) symbols). Discuss the

results. KS2: Carry out some addition and subtraction and then use the same figures as negative numbers. Discuss the results.

Geography
KS1: Make a map of the local area and mark out the customary way to get to certain places (e.g., shops, High Street, church). Then include some changes (e.g., road is closed for maintenance) and work out an alternative route. KS2: Using an OS map plot the *shortest* route to your diocesan cathedral. Then introduce some changes: plot the *quickest* route (possibly using a motorway or dual carriageway), and the most *scenic* route. Schools in a cathedral city should plot a course to another cathedral, or an abbey.

Changing circumstances (school assembly)

Nothing in life stays the same for long. We grow up and go to new schools, we move away and live somewhere else. As we grow older the changes get greater in our lives. All of us have to get accustomed to change and learn how to reorganize our lives when they change.

Play a game of cat and mouse. Using 9 (or 12) pupils, create three columns of three pupils (or three columns of four pupils). The pupils should hold hands with the person to the right and left of them. Appoint two other pupils as the cat and the mouse. The cat chases the mouse up and down the 'avenues' between the lines of pupils, or around the whole group.

At a given moment, shout 'change'. The 9 pupils then turn 90 degrees to their right and hold hands with the new people on their right and left. The cat and mouse will now find themselves in a different situation, and may suddenly be in the same row.

Play the game two or three times, emphasizing the word 'change' each time.

One of the biggest changes in the lives of the disciples was to occur 40 days after the resurrection. After his crucifixion by the Roman authorities, amazingly Jesus had reappeared to the disciples three days later, and although he seemed different to them, yet for the next few weeks he appeared to them, ate with them and taught them. However, the time was to come when Jesus was to leave them for good, and they would have to learn how to live without him. Acts 1.2b–11:

> Before [Jesus] . . . was taken up he gave instructions by the power of the Holy Spirit to the men he had chosen as his apostles. For forty days after his death he appeared to them many times in ways that proved beyond doubt that he was alive. They saw him, and he talked with them about the Kingdom of God. And when they came together, he gave them this order: 'Do not leave Jerusalem but wait for the gift I told you about, the gift my Father promised. John baptized with water, but in a few days you will be baptized with the Holy Spirit.' . . .
>
> 'When the Holy Spirit comes upon you, you will be filled with power, and you will be witnesses for me in Jerusalem, in all Judaea and Samaria, and to the ends of the earth.' After saying this, he was taken up to heaven as they watched him, and a cloud hid him from their sight.

For three years Jesus was with his disciples. They travelled throughout Israel, and he taught them everything. From the moment Jesus had appeared, their lives had changed. They had left their families and homes to follow him. They had seen sick people healed, the dead brought to life and thousands of people beginning to follow him.

Now for the first time the disciples have to learn how to manage without Jesus. In the past, when he went away to pray for a few hours, disaster overtook the disciples and they were unable to cope on their own. Now they must have wondered how they were going to manage without Jesus for good—even with the promise of the power of the Holy Spirit to help them. With Jesus gone, life was never to be the same again. However, he had left them a task. He had charged them with taking his message to the whole world.

Sometimes our lives too can change in dramatic ways. Perhaps we move house, or someone dies (or parents split up), or things we plan to do not work out. It can be quite difficult when this happens. But it is quite normal for our lives to change. Things do not stay the same for ever.

One of the things we can do when life seems about to change is to think of all the good things that the change might bring. This can be very helpful when we are trying to get accustomed to the change. (Give some examples of 'counting your blessings'. These might be: think how many new friends you might make when you move house; or, think of all the happy memories you have of the person who has died, etc.)

123

Lord God,
We thank you for the changes in our lives,
for new friends and new places to go.
Help us not to be afraid of change,
but to see that change can bring us new excitements,
new hope, and new joy. Amen.

 'You've got to move when the spirit says move' (*BBC Complete Come and Praise* 107)
'Spirit of God' (*BBC Complete Come and Praise* 63)

➡️ *RE*
Look at a number of the situations that children may face which can bring changes to their lives (e.g., moving to a new school, or the coming of a new brother or sister). KS2: Carry out some role-play to enable pupils to explore their feelings towards change.

English
KS1: Read *The Moving Mystery* by Carmen Harris. KS2: Read *Paper Faces* by Rachel Anderson.

History
KS1: Explore changes in the lives of pupils and their families (e.g., moving house, or the coming of a new brother or sister). Find out about the early lives of grandparents, etc. KS2: Explore change within the study unit being taught.

Geography
Explore the effect of water or wind, locally (e.g., river flooding, wind damage to buildings and trees). Investigate any local incidents. Alternatively, use CD-ROM or videos to obtain information.

Others who change (class assembly)

One of the hard lessons that children have to learn is that other people may be unreliable, and that they may change their minds. All of us have to learn how to cope with people who change.

Create some 'word ladders' that take pupils from one word to another. For instance, challenge pupils to change the word 'chin' to 'shop' by only changing one letter each time. Other examples are given below.

Example: *chin* to *shop*

    chin
    chip
    ship
    shop

Example: *letter* to *fatter*

    letter
    setter
    sitter
    fitter
    fatter

Example: *hill* to *dale*   Example: *file* to *dale*

hill	file
hall	fill
pall	hill
pale	hall
dale	tall
	tale
	dale

Alternatively, encourage pupils to create their own word ladders.

◆ Today's story from the Bible is about Moses and his brother Aaron. Moses had spent many weeks in the mountains talking with God, and God had given him a number of laws for the people to obey (the Ten Commandments). These were written down on large pieces of stone. The first law was 'I am the Lord your God . . . worship no God but me' (Exodus 19). Unfortunately, though, the people, led by Aaron, became fed-up with waiting for Moses. Exodus 32.1–10:

> When the people saw that Moses had not come down from the mountain but was staying there a long time, they gathered round Aaron and said to him, 'We do not know what has happened to this man Moses, who led us out of Egypt; so make us a god to lead us.'
>
> Aaron said to them, 'Take off the gold earrings which your wives, your sons, and your daughters are wearing, and bring them to me.' So all the people took off their gold earrings and brought them to Aaron. He took the earrings, melted them, poured the gold into a mould, and make a gold bull.
>
> The people said, 'Israel, this is our god, who led us out of Egypt!'
>
> Then Aaron built an altar in front of the gold bull and announced, 'Tomorrow there will be a festival to honour the Lord.' Early the next morning they brought some animals to burn as sacrifices and others to eat as fellowship offerings. The people sat down to a feast, which turned into an orgy of drinking. . . .
>
> The Lord said to Moses, 'Go back down at once, because your people, whom you led out of Egypt, have sinned and rejected me. They have already left the way that I commanded them to follow; they have made a bull out of melted gold and have worshipped it and offered sacrifices to it. They are saying that this is their god, who led them out of Egypt. I know how stubborn these people are. Now, don't try to stop

me. I am angry with them, and I am going to destroy them. Then I will make you and your descendants into a great nation.'

 Moses must have felt very badly let down by his brother, Aaron. Aaron was Moses' right-hand man, in charge of all the people of Israel. He was the man who had spoken for Moses to Pharaoh to get the Israelites freed. Moses trusted him more than anyone else. Yet it was Aaron who had let the people get out of control while Moses was in the mountains talking to God. It was he who had allowed the people to do something that he knew was wrong. The people of other nations made statues of their gods and worshipped them, but the Israelites had never been allowed to do this. Indeed the golden bull was the image used by a powerful tribe in the worship of their god, Baal.

Sometimes we too have friends or family who let us down. They are a little like the words on our word ladders! As we have seen, one word, with a few changes, can become another word. So one person can change into someone else.

However, we need to remember that both God and Moses forgave Aaron his mistake. He never forgot this lesson and was Moses' most loyal assistant to the end of his life.

RE
Explore how it feels to be let down by a friend. Read the next part of the story of Exodus. Who takes the blame for what has happened, and why?

Mathematics
Create grid patterns, with one or two mistakes. Use squared grid paper. Mark the squares vertically and horizontally with numbers. Give pupils the reference figures for an easy picture (perhaps a car or a house). Ask pupils to find the deliberate mistakes and correct them. Pupils might like to make their own pictures afterwards, and give the references to other class members to work out.

English
Read a story, or part of a story, that describes someone who changes (e.g., Edmund in the 'Snow Queen').

Science
KS1: Using mirrors, explore the similarities and differences between friends. Note similarities and differences in colouring, hair length, skin and eye colour, height and weight, etc. Produce artwork or written work for display. KS2: Extend the comparisons to other members of the family, looking at family characteristics (this will need sensitive handling particularly if there are adopted children in the class). What conclusions can be made, and how can they be displayed?

Art
Draw pictures of each other and display (see *Science*).

Change is great (class assembly)

Change can be exciting. We may not know what is around the corner, but when things change anything is possible. Children need to be enabled to see that change is not necessarily bad. It can also mean that our lives change for good.

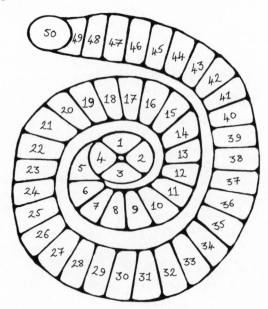

Create your own board game. Either use an existing board (like snakes and ladders) for the base, or make your own (see the suggestion in the picture above). The board should be numbered from 1 to at least 40. You will need a list of questions, two counters and a dice.

Offer to show pupils how good (or 'great') change can be. Choose two teams, of say six pupils in each team. Preferably choose confident pupils. Each team will have one counter between them, and questions are asked of the whole team—only one member should answer, but it can be any member of the team.

Alternatively, the whole class could play the game in groups of six. The game could be played over two or even three sessions. For KS1 pupils the board could have fewer numbers. Choose the easiest of questions, and explain as required.

Questions

    2. Who was your first friend?
    8. Remember something good about your first day at school.
  12. A new friend that you have made in the last year.
  13. A new member of the family that you like.
  16. A new game that you enjoyed.
  20. A good book that you have just read.
  21. A new group that you enjoy.
  25. Something different at home you like.
  26. A change at school that is fun.
  30. A new sport that you are enjoying playing or watching.
  32. Something new at school that you are enjoying.
  36. An animal friend you have made in the last year.
  38. Somewhere new you have been to that you enjoyed.
  40. A change you are looking forward to, when you become older.

Many, many years ago, a great change came to the people of Israel. They were defeated by the Babylonians, and the city of Jerusalem with its wonderful Temple was destroyed. The people must have thought that the end of the world had come as their Temple was looted and they were taken back to Babylon as slaves.

However, this situation did not last for long. Soon, another Empire was to arise—the Persian Empire—and things changed yet again. Ezra 1.1–4:

In the first year that Cyrus of Persia was emperor, the Lord made what he had said through the prophet Jeremiah come true. He prompted

Cyrus to issue the following command and send it out in writing to be read aloud everywhere in his empire:

'This is the command of Cyrus, Emperor of Persia. The Lord, the God of Heaven, has made me ruler over the whole world and has given me the responsibility of building a temple for him in Jerusalem in Judah. May God be with all of you who are his people. You are to go to Jerusalem and rebuild the Temple of the Lord, the God of Israel, the God who is worshipped in Jerusalem. If any of his people in exile need help to return, their neighbours are to give them this help. They are to provide them with silver and gold, supplies and pack animals, as well as offerings to present in the Temple of God in Jerusalem.'

As we have seen, many changes in our lives are good changes. We make new friends when we go to a new school or when we move house. We learn new things about ourselves and about others. Indeed, life can be quite exciting when things change.

The people in Jerusalem must have thought that things could not get better after they had been taken away from Jerusalem to Babylon. When the Persians came along they probably thought that they would still be treated like slaves. But instead the Persians freed the Israelites and sent them back to Jerusalem to rebuild the city and the Temple. This change was to be a great thing for the Israelites.

Lord God,
Sometimes we are worried about changes in our lives;
  help us to see that new things can be exciting.
If we are to grow we know we need to change;
  help us to be thoughtful when others find change difficult.
Keep us from staying where we are,
  because it is easier than making changes in our life. Amen.

English
Explore the letter E, and how it changes the way that other letters behave (e.g. hat/hate, bit/bite). Look at other vowels that carry out similar actions (e.g. *I* when applied to *A*).

Science
KS1: Look at objects and materials that can be changed (e.g., water, chocolate, bread). KS2: Look at growth and reproduction as appropriate, and specifically at the changes to the body that will occur at puberty.

History
Look at an everyday object like the telephone over the last 50 years, at the changes and improvements that have occurred.

RE
Explore the change that Jesus made to the lives of many of his followers (e.g., Matthew the tax-gatherer, Simon the Zealot, Mary Magdalene).

God is unchanging (school assembly)

Our world is constantly changing. Our lives change, friends change, and even we change. But God is unchanging. He loves his world and all its people. No matter what we do, God still loves us.

 Challenge pupils to think of any object in the world that does not change with time. You might like to start with some suggestions on a board. For example:

glass	gold
bricks	paper
water	clothing
stone	houses
toys	

You will need to think on your feet and to have answers ready, as some objects only change slightly over many years. For example, a gold ring wears down after many years of wearing; stone and slate may change in the face of volcanic action, etc.

◆ The Psalmists believed that the only thing in the universe that is unchanging is God. Many of the songs they wrote (the psalms) remind us that only God is unchanging. Psalm 146.1–6* (or 146.1–end):

Praise the Lord!
Praise the Lord, my soul!
I will praise him as long as I live;
I will sing to my God all my life.
Don't put your trust in human leaders;
no human being can save you.
When they die, they return to the dust;
on that day all their plans come to an end.

Happy is the man who has the God of Jacob to help him
and who depends on the Lord his God,
the Creator of heaven, earth, and sea,
and all that is in them.
He always keeps his promises;*
he judges in favour of the oppressed
and gives food to the hungry.

The Lord sets prisoners free
and gives sight to the blind.
He lifts those who have fallen;
he loves his righteous people.
He protects the strangers who live in our land;
he helps widows and orphans,
but ruins the plans of the wicked.

The Lord is king for ever.
Your God, O Zion, will reign for all time.

Praise the Lord!

◖ As we have seen, nothing in the world lasts for ever. We all grow older and change; the buildings and bridges we create get older and need repairing; even things like stone and slate change over time.

For Christians, God is the only thing that is unchanging in our world. He has always loved us, and continues to love us, no matter what we do. The men and women who wrote the psalms also knew this. In our psalm today we are reminded not to put our trust in people, but only in God. He is the only person who will not let us down.

'God who made the earth' (*BBC Complete Come and Praise* 10)
'All the nations of the earth' (*BBC Complete Come and Praise* 14)

Use pictures or artefacts to represent some of those things that God gives us (food, water, sunshine, love of family, love of friends, natural medicines, speech, sight, hearing, etc.).

Encourage silence as you talk of each thing that God has given to us. For example:

Lord God,
We thank you for the food that you give us,
the food we ate this morning, and will eat later today . . .
We thank you for our sight,
the beauty of hills and countryside, of rivers and of seas . . .

> *RE*
> The different Christian denominations emphasize different aspects of worship and of God. Look at what unites them: visit two different churches and encourage pupils to look at the churches to see what they have in common (possibly: altar, pulpit, pews, etc). KS2: Look at baptism in the Baptist Church and in the Church of England. What are the similarities, what are the differences, and why?
>
> *Science*
> Explore the changing movement of the sun and its effects. On a sunny day draw the position of the sun at different times of the day (ensuring that pupils do not look directly at the sun). Plot the movement of shadows during the day and find out when the shadows were shortest and when longest.
>
> *Art*
> Create motifs and patterns out of circles (which have no beginning and no end, and are unchanging!). Look at Celtic or Islamic work and create patterns in a similar style. KS2: Use patterns in the dyeing of material.
>
> *Mathematics*
> Explore numerical patterns that never change.

ENDINGS

Endings, like beginnings, are a normal part of human life. Unfortunately, many of us try to avoid thinking too much about the end of a friendship, or the end of our time at school. We particularly do not like to think of the end of our time on earth. Children need to be helped to see that endings are a natural part of life, and lead on to new experiences. In fact they always lead on to the beginning of something else.

Where are we going? (school assembly)

We are all travelling on a journey—the journey of life. To travel means that we ought to know where we are going. We should have some end in sight. This assembly looks at possible endings.

Role-play two adults going on holiday in a car. The usual chaos ensues: suitcases and bags are gathered in a pile where someone falls over them; ('Have the hot water bottles been put in?'); there is no more room in the cases but space is needed for . . . ; has the water been turned off? have the windows been locked? have the plants in the bathroom been watered? does the milkman know not to call?

After some time the couple finish loading the car and step inside. The engine is turned on, they negotiate their way out onto the main road ('Is there anything coming?'), and set off with general conversation about how wonderful the holiday will be. They travel some distance, perhaps beginning to think of having a rest or a drink, when they discover that neither of them know where they are actually going! They do not know the address or village where they are to stay!

It is absolutely no good going on holiday if you have no idea where you are going. When we travel anywhere we always need to know our destination, otherwise we would end up travelling in circles.

Life is just like this. We are travelling on the journey of life, and we need to have some idea of where we are going and what might lie ahead.

Obviously we cannot map out our exact route in life, because unexpected things happen. But we still need to aim for somewhere.

Christians know where they are going in life because Jesus told them exactly the way to go. Jesus taught them that this life is like a journey back to God. He said that if they believed in him, and followed his commands then they would know the way to travel.

 This is what Jesus told his disciples. John 14.2, 4, 5–6, 14:

'There are many rooms in my Father's house, and I am going to prepare a place for you. I would not tell you this if it were not so . . . You know the way that leads to the place where I am going.'

Thomas said to him, 'Lord, we do not know where you are going; so how can we know the way to get there?'

Jesus answered him, 'I am the way, the truth, and the life; no one goes to the Father except by me . . . If you ask for anything in my name, I will do it.'

 'Travel on' (*BBC Complete Come and Praise* 42)
'The journey of life' (*BBC Complete Come and Praise* 45)

 Mention, first, that the word *Amen* means, *So be it*. In other words we are agreeing to what is said when we say *Amen*.

Leader: Lord God,
     On our journey of life let us not forget others who travel with us.
All: Amen.
Leader: On our journey of life let us not stand still for too long.
All: Amen.
Leader: On our journey of life keep us always looking ahead.
All: Amen.
Leader: On our journey bring us at the last to you.
All: Amen.

➡ *Geography*
KS1: Make maps of a real or imagined journey, using pictures and symbols. The map could be of a journey undertaken in a story book. KS2: Plan a journey abroad, create a map using symbols and a key. If possible give grid references.

English
Read a story about a personal journey of growth (e.g., *Climbing Father's Mountain* by W. J. Corbett).

History
Within the topic being studied, look at modes of transport, journey times, places travelled to, difficulties to be overcome, costumes worn, etc.

RE
Read about Jonah, who tried to escape from God and travel where he wanted to travel. Or talk about life as a journey (see page 33 of the Report *Children in the Way* (NS/CHP) which likened our journey to a walk, where some stop to admire the view, others rush on to see what is around the corner, and yet others carry small children who are tired or wait with the elderly).

Art
Create artwork based on the story of Jonah and the whale.

Getting to the end of the journey (school)

This assembly looks at the kind of path we travel in life, at some of the obstacles that lay in wait, and of our eventual arrival at our journey's end.

✎ Make a large map (on a whiteboard or on paper), with at least four routes for a traveller to take between two imaginary towns. Put in two towns and the winding routes of four roads connecting them. All four roads are different lengths, but at least one should appear much longer. All routes should pass close by one of the following: a casino, a pub, someone selling drugs, a quarry with a 'no swimming' sign. The routes should be numbered 1 to 4.

Create some obstacles to be encountered on the journey and draw (or write) these on pieces of paper (e.g., a large lake which has to be skirted or overcome; a bog; a mountain; a wide river; a bandit hideout; a town). Place the pictures in four envelopes. Number the envelopes 1, 2, 3 and 4.

Make up a story about four people (all adults) travelling from one town to the other. Give them names, characters and reasons for travelling. Emphasize that all four need to get to the other town as quickly as possible.

Then ask four pupils to help you. They are to decide which route they would travel *in order to get to the town as quickly as possible*. Give each pupil who chooses a road an envelope. If desired place figures on the routes, and describe what happens to each person as they meet the obstacles. Three of the travellers get side-tracked by betting, swimming, drugs or drinking. The fourth does not choose to get side-tracked from the path.

Three of the travellers do not arrive, having been defeated by the obstacles or side-tracked by the amusements. But the one who takes the most unappealing route (i.e., the longest route) arrives first, not having deviated from the route marked out.

 Jesus had something to say about the journey we travel. He talked about the journey not as a road, but as a gate. Matthew 7.13–14, 21:

'Go in through the narrow gate, because the gate to hell is wide and the road that leads to it is easy, and there are many who travel it. But the gate to life is narrow and the way that leads to it is hard, and there are few people who find it . . .

Not everyone who calls me "Lord, Lord" will enter the Kingdom of heaven, but only those who do what my Father in heaven wants them to do.'

Every day of our life we have to make choices, and it can be very difficult. Sometimes we choose the most attractive option and find that it wasn't a good choice after all.

All the travellers in the story suddenly found their roads had lots of obstacles. But three of them got side-tracked by other things, and did not keep on travelling. So although they all needed to end up at ____ (city name), unfortunately they didn't manage to get there. Only ____ (name of person travelling on route 4) arrived at his/her destination.

Each of us needs to think carefully about the way we travel in life if we want to arrive at our destination—to be where God is (the place we call Heaven). We need to think about the choices we make each day and be sure that they are choices that God would approve.

Jesus taught us to love one another, to help one another, and to think of others before we think of ourselves. If we obey these commands we should not find ourselves straying off the path, and one day we should find ourselves at our journey's end, with God.

 'I am planting my feet in the footsteps' (*BBC Complete Come and Praise* 103)
'I may speak in the tongues of angels' (*BBC Complete Come and Praise* 100)

 Lord God,
Sometimes we are not sure which way to travel,
and which choices to make.
Help us to choose wisely,
and to travel carefully,
so that one day we may return to be where you are,
in your kingdom of peace and love. Amen.

RE
Read a paraphrase of the story of *Pilgrim's Progress* by John Bunyan, or look at some of the obstacles that he had to overcome. KS2: Discuss what are the equivalent figures today to the following: Mr Pliable, Mr Worldly Wiseman, Faithful, the Evangelist.

History
Look at the life and work of a famous person involved in inventing a modern means of travel, particularly one appropriate to the area in which the school is based (e.g., a steamship, airplane, car, train). What were the difficulties involved for the inventor and how were they overcome? Were there any accidents in the early days? Where did people travel at the time of the period being studied?

Geography
KS1: Use globes, maps and plans—in a variety of scales—to plan ways of travelling between different towns or countries. Identify possible major landscape difficulties in the way, and negotiate a way round them. KS2: Plan journeys from one country to another, via a third country, identifying and avoiding landscape features that might cause difficulties. Create maps, and work out grid references, if desired.

PE
Hold a scavenger hunt in the school grounds, or some other suitable place, giving pupils a limited time to find the items required so that they will need to keep active physically.

Moving away (class assembly)

Many children in today's world have to move homes and leave their present school and friends. It can be a very traumatic time for them. This assembly helps them to think through the move so that they can better face the event if it should occur to them.

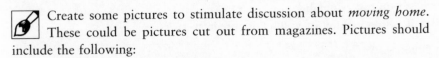 Create some pictures to stimulate discussion about *moving home*. These could be pictures cut out from magazines. Pictures should include the following:

- a school
- a typical boy's/girl's bedroom
- two children playing (in a playground/skating/swimming, etc.)
- two children talking
- a church
- shops in a town/countryside/seaside (as appropriate to your school)
- a blank piece of paper.

Divide the class into small groups. Inform the groups that they are to think about moving home. Comment that many children have to move home at some time or other (perhaps their parent(s) get a new job), and some will move home many times. Ask how many children have moved home already.

Add that the pictures are to remind them of some of the things they might miss if they had to move home. Ask them to talk together about what they might miss most, and then to decide between them in which order they would place the pictures (No. 1 will be what they miss most). The blank piece of paper allows an extra choice, if desired.

The groups should try to come to a consensus if possible. If this is not possible, allow the pupils to create their own lists.

The people of Israel knew all about moving home and how sad it made them. Here are two songs they sang after they were taken away to be in exile in Babylon. Psalm 137.1–6 and Psalm 42.5:

Psalm 137.1–6

> By the rivers of Babylon we sat down;
> there we wept when we remembered Zion.
> On the willows near by
> we hung up our harps.
> Those who captured us told us to sing;
> they told us to entertain them:
> 'Sing us a song about Zion'.
> How can we sing a song to the Lord
> in a foreign land?
> May I never be able to play the harp again
> if I forget you, Jerusalem!
> May I never be able to sing again
> if I do not remember you,
> if I do not think of you as my greatest joy!

Psalm 42.5

> Why am I so sad?
> Why am I so troubled?
> I will put my hope in God,
> and once again I will praise him,
> my saviour and my God.

The Jewish people were defeated in battle by the Babylonians. The city of Jerusalem with its wonderful Temple was destroyed, and most of the people who had not been killed were taken away to Babylon as slaves. This song shows how dreadfully upset they were at having to leave their home city of Jerusalem, and to live so far away.

Everyone has to move home at some time in their life. It can be hard, because we miss our friends (and sometimes family) very much.

Comment on the conclusions pupils reached about those things they would miss most. Add that although we shall miss home, and our friends, when we move we quickly make a new home and find more friends. We may miss the countryside (or town, or seaside), but there will be new places to explore and new adventures awaiting us. Indeed, even the people of Israel did not stay in Babylon for ever. Eventually they came back to Israel, and in the meantime, as we saw, they turned to God for comfort.

Pray for any pupils who will be moving home and school in the near future, and for those who may be moving into the district and/or school where you live.

Lord God,
We thank you for our homes and families,
for our school, and for our town (or the countryside or the seaside).
So often we take them all for granted.
Help us to appreciate them this day.
We pray for ____ (or *all*) who will be leaving us soon,
and for ____ (or *all*) who will be moving into this area,
and ask that you will keep them safe and protect them. Amen.

Music
Learn the song 'By the waters of Babylon'.

English
Read *The Moving Mystery* by Carmen Harris or *There's No Such Place as Far Away* by Richard Bach. Produce a newspaper, using the computer, on the subject of Moving.

IT
Appoint writers, artists and cartoonists to produce work for the newspaper. Appoint an Editor or Editorial Team to oversee the production of the newspaper (see *English*).

RE
Read about the end of Jerusalem, the attack and exile by the Babylonians, and their subsequent return (2 Chronicles 36.11–end). Find out about the building of the first Temple (1 Kings 5–8) and the

rebuilding of the Temple (Ezra). (Pictures of the later Temple can usually be found in any modern Bible.)

Design Technology
Design and plan a Temple for Jerusalem. If desired, working in small groups, build the finished product.

Mathematics/Art
Design and plan the Temple to scale, and produce plans (see *Design Technology*).

The end of life (class)

Many people find it hard to think about death, but children need to begin to accept that death, like birth, is a natural part of life. All things that live, die. Those who prefer to push the thought of death away are already beginning to create for themselves a mental block about the subject. So this assembly gently attempts to encourage pupils to think about the end of life.

Create small groups of pupils and give each group a simple puzzle. The puzzles should only take five or ten minutes to complete (depending on the time allowed for the class assembly). Each puzzle should have one piece missing from the centre of the picture—which you hold back.

When the puzzles are completed (with the exception of the missing pieces), sympathize with each group that there is a missing piece, commenting that 'It's not finished' and that 'It's difficult to see what all the picture is about'.

Alternatively, tell a short and exciting story, but refrain from giving the ending of the story.

The theme for this assembly is 'The end of life'. The puzzles (or story) are rather like our lives. At present there are some missing pieces, because we are only half-way finished—we haven't completed our life as yet.

When there are missing pieces from a jigsaw we cannot see the full picture. It is hard to see if we are going to like the picture or not. It is even hard sometimes to see what the picture is about. We need the missing pieces to completely finish the jigsaw (or, we need the end of the story to complete the story). Without the missing pieces there is no ending.

Our lives are just like this. Only when our lives are completely finished will it be possible to see the whole picture. The ending of our life is just as natural as the beginning of our life.

We do not know what will happen after death or when we shall die, but Jesus did promise us that if we believe in him we should be with him in his Father's house. So the next life should be even better than this life.

Jesus teaches his disciples about heaven. John 14.1–3.

'Do not be worried and upset,' Jesus told them. 'Believe in God and believe also in me. There are many rooms in my Father's house, and I am going to prepare a place for you. I would not tell you this if it were not so. And after I go and prepare a place for you, I will come back and take you to myself, so that you will be where I am.'

 Finally, give each group the missing piece of jigsaw (or tell pupils the end of the story), and comment that now we can see the whole picture.

Encourage pupils to write their own prayers—perhaps for those who are elderly and nearing the end of their lives. Alternatively, encourage pupils to talk through what they might want to ask God, and then sum up their thoughts in a prayer, using some of their own words.

RE
KS1: Read *Waterbugs and Dragonflies* by Doris Stickney, and gently answer any questions the pupils may have. KS2: Read *Badger's Parting Gifts* by Susan Varley. What gifts would pupils like to leave to their friends and family?

Invite someone to come and to talk to your class, or the whole school, from a local Hospice.

Art
Pose the question: If death was a colour what colour would it be? Encourage pupils to express themselves on the subject of death in whatever colour seems appropriate to them. KS2: Make observations, in the form of drawings, of plants (see *Science*).

Music
Consider the kind of music suitable for a funeral. Play Purcell's *Queen Mary's Funeral Music*. This was also played at Purcell's own funeral a few months after it was first written. Does this always have to be solemn? What might be played today?

Science
KS1: Look at life cycles in the insect world. Keep mealworms or study another life cycle (e.g., frogs or mice). KS2: Look at the life cycle of a flowering plant. Explore the differences between flowers using hand lenses. Make observations, and name as many parts of the flower as possible.

End of year/leaving school (school assembly)

The way that we end the school year (or school life) is important. There should be time for reflection and an acknowledgement of what was worthwhile. Sometimes we may wish to carry on a symbol of the old life into the new one. At other times it is sufficient to reflect on what has happened. Endings, as with beginnings, quickly acquire traditional ceremonies and customs. This assembly enables pupils to offer ceremonially the last year or the last few years, and to move on to the new year or new school.

Encourage pupils to bring forward items that symbolize the different parts of their school life (football, artwork, design and technology projects, etc). If pupils are leaving school at this time, they might wish to present items to represent all the stages of their school life. Allow individuals, or small groups, to come forward to talk about the significance of the items they offer, and the memories they recall.

After the Jews had been freed from Egypt, God commanded them to remember the day that he freed them from Pharaoh by holding the festival of Unleavened Bread each year. Exodus 13.3–10:

Moses said to the people, 'Remember this day—the day on which you left Egypt, the place where you were slaves. This is the day the Lord brought you out by his great power. No leavened bread is to be eaten. You are leaving Egypt on this day in the first month, the month of Abib. The Lord solemnly promised your ancestors to give you the land of the Canaanites, the Hittites, the Amorites, the Hivites, and the Jebusites. When he brings you into that rich and fertile land, you must celebrate this festival in the first month of every year. For seven days you must eat unleavened bread and on the seventh day there is to be a festival to honour the Lord. For seven days you must not eat any bread made with yeast; there must be no yeast or leavened bread anywhere in your land. When the festival begins, explain to your sons that you do all this because of what the Lord did for you when you left Egypt. This observance will be a reminder, like something tied on your hand or on your forehead; it will remind you to continue to recite and study the Law of the Lord, because the Lord brought you out of Egypt by his great power. Celebrate this festival at the appointed time each year.'

Jews still remember the time when God freed them from slavery in Egypt, even though this happened many thousands of years ago. Each year they hold a special meal (a Passover meal) to remember when God 'passed over' them and they and their children were saved, while the Egyptians were punished for their disobedience.

At the Passover meal Jews eat unleavened bread (bread without yeast in it to make it rise), and bitter herbs, and read again the story of what happened all those years ago.

We may not eat a meal to remember our life at school (although some schools do), but we can use items (or 'symbols') to remind us of the good and bad times we have had here over the last year (or years), and of what we have learnt about ourselves, about the world, and about each other. Like the Jews we use these symbols to tell ourselves the stories of what we have been doing in school.

All our experiences, whether they were good or bad, will be useful in the future. The things that happen help to make us into the kind of people we shall become. God wants us to grow into loving men and women, who care about other people. At the end of each year (or school life) it is therefore very important that we think back over our time here, to find out what we have learnt—not just in history or maths, but about ourselves and about other people, so that we can try and put it into practice when we start the next year (or school).

'Shalom' (*BBC Complete Come and Praise* 141)
'Round, round, round' (*BBC Complete Come and Praise* 111)
'You shall go out with joy' (*BBC Complete Come and Praise* 98)

Ask pupils to help by bringing forward items already mentioned.

Leader: Lord God,
This ____ (pupil holds up one item: e.g., a flash-card word or a Maths book)
reminds me of ____ ('the first words we learnt, or the time we learnt about . . .)
All: We thank you, Lord.
Leader: Lord God,
This ____
reminds me of ____ etc.
All: We thank you, Lord.

History
Revise topics learnt this year, perhaps through the means of a quiz.

English
Choose a positive incident from the past year/years and role-play what happened. Do memories of the incident differ between different pupils?

Art
Draw or paint symbols to represent incidents or subjects learnt this year, or in previous years.

RE
Explore symbols of God (perhaps those important when pupils were younger, or those important now). Discuss what might be a symbol for God (e.g., a cross, an old man, the sun).

Alternatively, working in pairs, encourage pupils to explore what they like about their friends/one another, and to thank them for all that they have meant over the past year/years.

Useful Addresses

World development

Christian Aid
PO Box 100
London
SE1 7RT

Catholic Fund for Overseas Development (CAFOD)
2 Romero Close
London
SW9 9TY

One World Week
PO Box 100
London
SE1 7RT

Oxfam
274 Banbury Road
Oxford
OX2 7DZ

Save the Children
Education Unit
17 Grove Lane
London
SE5 8RD

UNICEF
25 Churchgater
Leicester
LE1 3AL

World Development Movement (WDM)
25 Beehive Place
London
SW9 7QR

Church overseas

Church Missionary Society (CMS)
157 Waterloo Road,
London
SE1 8UU

Leprosy Mission
Goldhay Way
Orton Goldhay
Peterborough
PE2 5GZ

Society for Promoting Christian Knowledge (SPCK)
Holy Trinity Church
Marylebone Road
London
NW1 4DU

South American Missionary Society (SAMS)
Allen Gardiner House
Pembury Road
Tunbridge Wells
Kent TN2 3QU

United Society for the Propagation of the Gospel (USPG)
157 Waterloo Road
London
SE1 8XA

Environment

Friends of the Earth (FOE)
26–28 Underwood Street
London
N1 7JQ

Greenpeace
Canonbury Villas
London
N1 2PN

Prisoners of conscience

Amnesty International
99 Roseberry Avenue
London
EC1 4RE

Race

Campaign for Racial Equality
Elliott House
Allington Street
London
SW1E 7EH

Poverty

Child Poverty Action Group
1 Bath Street
London
EC1V 9DX

Christian Action
St Anselm's Church Hall
Kennington Cross
Kennington Road
London
SE11 5DU

Families

Exploring Parenthood
Latimer Education Centre
194 Freston Road
London
W10 6TT

Family Life and Marriage Education (FLAME)
11 Mundy Street
Heanor
Derbyshire
DE7 7EB

Gingerbread
35 Wellington Street
London
WC2E 7BN

The Mothers' Union
Mary Sumner House
24 Tufton Street
London
SW1P 3RB

National Council for One Parent Families
255 Kentish Town Road
London
NW5 2LX

Stepfamily
72 Willesden Lane
London
NW6 7TA

Consumer products

Fairtrade Foundation
Suite 204/5
16/16a Baldwin's Gardens
London
EC1N 7RT

Traidcraft
Kingsway
Gateshead
NE11 0NE

Book List

Hymn Book

BBC Complete Come and Praise (BBC 1990)

Other books referred to

Rachel Anderson, *Paper Faces* (Oxford University Press 1997)
Richard Bach, *There's No Such Place as Far Away* (HarperCollins 1993)
Frances Hodgson Burnett, *The Secret Garden* (Hodder & Stoughton 1994)
Children in the Way (National Society/Church House Publishing 1998)
Peter Churchill, *Feeling Good* (National Society/Church House Publishing 1994)
W. J. Corbett, *Hamish Climbing Father's Mountain* (Hodder & Stoughton 1995)
Robert Cormier, *Other Bells for Us to Ring* (HarperCollins 1994)
The Dramatised Bible (Hodder & Stoughton 1997)
Mick Gower, *Jimmy Woods and the Big Bad Wolf* (A&C Black Publishers Ltd 1994)
Carmen Harris, *The Moving Mystery* (Heinemann 1990)
Jeremie Hughes, *Will My Rabbit Go to Heaven?* (Lion 1988)
Arnold Kellet, *Ee by Gum, Lord* (Smith Settle 1996)
Dick King-Smith, *Friends and Brothers* (Mammoth 1989)
Dick King-Smith, *Omnibombulator* (Doubleday 1995)
Carolyn Nystrom, *The Lark Who Had No Song* (Lion 1991)
Carolyn Nystrom, *Emma Says Goodbye* (Lion 1990)
Brian Sibley, *The Frightful Food Feud* (Lion 1994)
Carolyn Sloan, *Helen Keller* (Evans Bros 1992)
Doris Stickney *Waterbugs and Dragonflies* (Mowbray 1996)
Susan Varley, *Badger's Parting Gifts* (Collins 1992)